SUCCESS Secrets OF ENTREPRENEURS

JEREMY CASSELL . MINDY GIBBINS-KLEIN .
JON KEEL . NICK MARANGOS . JAY MOORE .
ANDREW MORGAN . CHRIS O'HARE .
OWEN O'MALLEY . STEVE SANDERS .
SUBASH TAVARES . LESLEY THOMAS .
MATT THOMPSETT .

a Re think Press company

First published in 2022 by
Panoma Press Ltd
www.rethinkpress.com
www.panomapress.com

Book layout by Neil Coe

978-1-784529-72-7

CONTENTS

FOREWORD

'A clever man knows what he wants; a wise man knows what he doesn't want.'

- Jack Ma

I guess there are not many 'entrepreneurs' who have achieved the heights of risk, sacrifice and sheer determination of 'keeping going' like Jack Ma and Elon Musk. Many of us are in danger of saying 'He got lucky' or 'I wish I could be as successful as Elon Musk'. We have to remember they have trodden the same path as you, perhaps on a larger scale; however, the roller coaster will be a similar ride.

We have met many entrepreneurs that use a benchmark like Elon Musk or other massive 'tech billionaires'. Yet is this helpful? The principle of Business is Personal (BIP) is that we each must create our own unique recipe for our definition of success; your business is personal to you. This is a belief we have held ever since we chose that path ourselves in the 1990s.

There are many roads we can take to having a sense of fulfilment and success, and those of us who have chosen to be an entrepreneur have not chosen an easy road. What drives us to do this? Is it our desire for complete independence and self-reliance? Is it personal impact, or is it just the thrill of this ride?

Within the pages of this book are 12 entrepreneurs who have trodden the path and remain convinced and passionate about this way of managing our personal needs in life. To be an entrepreneur is a joy and a curse; each day offers new learning and new challenges to overcome.

There are many theories shared; listen to the journeys which have provided them all with a strong desire to pass on wisdom. The culture of this book is one of friendship. This is the opportunity to sit down with a friend in business and listen to their beliefs and wisdom. To take some nuggets away with you, some of which you will action.

Each author is an expert in their niche. Some have shared their precise expertise, and some have talked more about the beliefs they have as an entrepreneur. Enjoy the words from Andrew Morgan, encouraging you to focus on three aspects of business survival; be inspired by Chris O'Hare through his devotion to your need to 'think like a tech company'. Feel the passion in Jay Moore's words around the 'real power of connecting with others'.

Consider some practical aspects of your business, such as the wisdom of Jeremy Cassell, sharing his '12 Habits of Exceptional Presenting', and the wise words of Nick Marangos around the critical nature of how we approach scaling our business through recruitment.

Laugh with Matt Thompsett through his words 'You are probably crazy', offering a few truths and ideas around being an entrepreneur. Alongside Matt's thoughts, enjoy the experience of Jon Keel, who shares his recipe for building a successful career as a serial business builder.

Let's not forget our mindset. Do you have the right 'Money Mindset'? Lesley Thomas provides valuable words for us all to consider, a massive mindset block that we can unlock. Jump into the chapter by Mindy Gibbins-Klein and see the world through the lens of 'thought leadership'. Could you be a thought leader? Or perhaps you don't want to be, so, how about coaching someone in your business to be your 'known', respected 'thought leader' in your sector?

How about the strategy you take to build assets in your life? How do you improve your business valuation right from the start with Steve Sanders as your guide? Finally, consider this, is it a good idea to invest in other entrepreneurs to spread your risk? A methodology and inspirational thinking from Owen O'Malley to motivate you to learn the stock market.

This book is packed with short, digestible, impactful thoughts. You can read the chapters in any order. We hope it becomes a companion; our shared desire is that the authors feel like your friends. Most of all, we all wish you joy, success, and health, we admire you, and we are sitting right next to you as you flick through these pages. Your friend, as business is personal, and we care.

Thomas Power and Penny Power OBE

The 12 Habits Of Exceptional Presenters

JEREMY CASSELL

I have a simple mindset about presenting – exceptional presenters are made, not born. Everything included in this chapter is learnable.

As an entrepreneur, you deliver both formal and informal presentations, either internally within your organisation or externally, as part of your never-ending business development efforts. These opportunities are often high-stakes presentations because it is critical for you to engage, motivate or gain commitment, not just inform. Think about all those entrepreneurial moments when presentation skills are essential: pitches to land high profile investors, partners or customers, internal training to motivate staff, and external conference keynotes. During the startup phase, being capable of bringing investors and customers on board is essential to your survival; in the growth phase, being able to keep your vision alive and gain new, enthusiastic supporters allows you to grow and prosper. Done well, these presentations can be transformational. Done badly, they can be cringeworthy and damage your reputation.

What are the positive habits that make the real difference? I have worked with numerous leaders and 'C Suite' executives and have co-authored *The Leader's Guide to Presenting*, which was the UK Business Book of the Year in 2018. The truth is that outstanding presenters share 12 habits. Integrating these best practice habits into your own approach to presenting will allow you to step up from good to exceptional, reduce any stress you feel around public speaking and guarantee that your presentations hit the mark every time.

Here is a quick-fire, practical overview of my 12 habits, which will give you the know-how to take your entrepreneurial presenting to the next level.

Habit 1: Keep your audience at the heart of every presentation

Every presentation must be audience centric. Too many business presentations are the exact opposite: presenter centric. Nobody likes being sold to, so make the client the hero. Deliver presentations centred around the audience and help solve their pain points; engagement then is inevitable. Your job is to build trust in your core messages so you can guide them to the promised land. Prepare with the audience in mind, identify how you offer real value and then focus on creating a connection. This is the first and most important habit.

Habit 2: Consistently follow a preparation model

Never be tempted to 'wing it'. Having your personal process in place will allow you to feel more confident and save you time. Here is my preparation framework that I use every time:

1. **Identify audience needs.** Put yourself in their shoes – what is the knowledge level? What are their priorities? How motivated are they to listen? What are the core messages that are likely to resonate? Build your presentation around your analysis.

2. **Set outcome.** As an entrepreneur, you are likely to be presenting in order to motivate, get your audience thinking, train, persuade, instruct or inform. Link your goal to actions you want the audience to take as a result of attending.

3. **Brainstorm.** Get creative and suspend judgment.

4. **Structure.** Select your key messages & develop your narrative.

5. **Create a compelling start and finish.**

6. **Rehearse.** Properly. Every time – no excuses!

7. **Access your resourceful state.** Take time to get into a confident flow state.

Habit 3: Be aware of mindset and manage your state

Public speaking is something many fear – even visionary CEOs. Tesla's Elon Musk, for example, has publicly chastised himself for his lacklustre performances, most notably at a 2011 SpaceX Press conference during which he blunders, stutters and fluffs his lines.

I see too many presentations in which the presenter isn't in control. Nerves, fear, negative thought patterns have taken over. You need to take responsibility and find a way to present without fear. You *can* reduce unnecessary anxiety and deliver in what I call a 'coherent' state. Essentially this means being in harmony with yourself. Self-awareness is the first step towards eliminating unhelpful mental or behavioural habits. Coherence is a habit as well as a positive, resourceful state in which to present. Any entrepreneur can access this resourceful state in a myriad of ways – for example, by using specific breathing patterns, reframing nerves into excitement and by power posing (see Amy Cuddy).

Habit 4: Structure every presentation

'If you can't explain it simply, you don't understand it well enough.'

– Albert Einstein

Distil your content rather than subject your audience to an information dump. Less is more. Your presentation must be easily understood. George Miller wrote a paper in 1956 in which he postulated that in a short period of time, most people cannot take in more than 7, plus/minus 2, chunks of information. So – an absolute maximum of nine key points. For a short presentation, utilise the power of three (or Tricolon, in ancient rhetoric). This idea is based on the fact that information grouped in threes is more memorable and persuasive. Think of comedy catchphrases, marketing and political slogans. For example, 'education, education, education', 'Stay home, protect the NHS, save lives' and 'Suit you, sir'. I built an influencing model with Tom Bird called The C^3 Model of Influencing – Confidence, Credibility and Connection. Three key points are easy to remember for us as the presenter as well as the audience. So 'Just Do It'.

Habit 5: Present with authenticity

Authenticity in presenting is the interconnection between what you are saying, how you are saying it, and what you believe. Be true to yourself, just with more skill! Instead of giving a one-way presentation, you are having a conversation with your audience. This personal approach makes giving presentations much easier. You don't have to memorise a 'produced talk'. You can just be yourself and talk as if you are having a conversation with your friends. What is interesting is that by just being yourself, you usually stand out. Your energy and passion will make you different and memorable.

Habit 6: Articulate a burning platform

Your audience needs a compelling reason to listen to you if you are asking them to change their approach. They need to understand why the change is so important. Focus on the why – why should your audience listen to you?

Failure to present a compelling reason for change is likely to lead the audience to not seeing change as a key priority. Everyone in your audience has both away from (pain) and towards (pleasure) motivations. You may therefore need to signpost the positive consequences of achieving the change as well as the negative consequences of not taking action. Use Power Words such as save, solve, increase, improve and reduce to emphasise the benefits of change.

Habit 7: Deliver a compelling start and finish

We've all seen those presenters who, the minute they walk on stage, cause the entire audience to sit up straight and lean forward in their chairs. Too many entrepreneurs sabotage their chances by delivering anodyne beginnings to presentations. I have consistently seen business presenters ease into their presentations at the start, and some of my coachees and training attendees have even admitted to me something along the lines of, 'If I can just get through the first 2-3 minutes, then I tend to settle down'.

The truth? If you don't do the right things at the start, you will very often have already lost the audience. Your audience is likely to remember the start and the finish, so make them count. It is the idea of primacy and recency. Here is how you start a presentation.

INTRO – Interest, Need, Title, Range, Objectives

Interest – What can you do to capture interest immediately? I always use a spike. This was coined by Graham Davies in his book The Presentation Coach. A spike is a sentence or series of short sentences that gets to the heart of your messaging. Dame Anita Roddick said, 'If you think you're too small to make an impact, try going to bed with a mosquito.'

Here are two examples of spikes created by leaders I have worked with:

- 'There are 70 harvests left in the world'

- 'We are a Top 10 law firm'

Need – Why does your audience need to be there? One of the main reasons people don't engage well with presenters is that they don't always clearly understand why they are there. Ensure you describe an issue or the reasons why people need the information you are about to give them.

Title – I see so many boring titles, so make yours catchy! And the second T – cover off timings.

Range – Establish that your presentation has a clear agenda and share it.

Objectives – What will your audience know, understand and be able to do after you have finished?

Have the final word – make a last point, after questions, to leave a lasting impression. Finish with a call to action and own the final flourish.

Habit 8: Engage the audience as much as possible

When you are presenting online, there are multiple distractions – your audience can be tempted with messaging, social media, eating, you name it! Whether it is virtual or face to face, you have to engage the audience. Here are a few engagement ideas:

- Ask rhetorical questions.

- Utilise both the credible and connection voice patterns. The credible voice pattern is slow, monotone, uses pauses and goes down at the end of a sentence or phrase (think Barack Obama). The connection pattern is the exact opposite – fast, no pauses, vocal variety and upward inflection (think Julie Walters).

- Illustrate your presentation with compelling, colourful and sensory-specific language, rather than the (often) digital language I see employed by entrepreneurs.

- Tell stories. People like surprises, suspense and drama. So, connect through the stories or metaphors you use about your career, your expertise and your clients.

Virtually, I always use Mentimeter – this is interactive engagement software that works superbly to keep the audience interested through questions and polling.

Habit 9: Provide compelling and credible evidence

Using evidence and logic will increase your credibility as a presenter. Never assume that your audience thinks you are credible.

People are persuaded by both logic and emotion. You need both to deliver an exceptional presentation. Focus on finding a few *relevant* pieces of evidence (facts, statistics, objective criteria) to support your core messages, rather than a slew of facts that are loosely related to your main point.

Habit 10: Encourage and manage audience questions

During preparation, ask yourself, 'What are the five worst questions I really don't want to be asked?' Prepare answers for these. Having a simple structure increases your ability to answer questions effectively. This is why I created the 4 A approach:

1. **A**cknowledge the question.

2. Throw it open to the **A**udience (when possible).

3. **A**nswer – bottom line your response.

4. **A**sk the questioner if the question has been answered.

Answering questions effectively is where you really earn your crust as a presenter.

Habit 11: Practise on the edge of discomfort

You do not develop skills by building knowledge. There are numerous forums and opportunities for entrepreneurs to practise presenting. Have you heard the legendary Gary Player golfing story? He holed a bunker shot in competition. Afterwards, an interviewer suggested it was luck. His reply was, 'Strangely, the more I practise, the luckier I get'. The more you practise presenting (with awareness and feedback), the more your reputation will grow as a presenter.

Habit 12: Accept all feedback dispassionately

There is no such thing as a perfect presentation, and there are always ways to change and improve. There is no failure, only feedback. Many virtual presentations are recorded nowadays, so it is straightforward enough to review your presentations and get feedback. Ask yourself, 'What worked? What could I have done differently?'

Ideally, hire a coach like me to help you! Try not to react emotionally to critical feedback – learn from it instead and develop your own emotional intelligence.

Together, these 12 habits provide a strong foundation from which you can develop your own authentic voice and presentation style as an entrepreneur. Use them as a template to develop your positive presenting habits. Do you now believe you are capable of delivering consistently exceptional presentations?

Jeremy Cassell coaches leaders who want to present, influence and build business with more confidence and authenticity. He helps them deliver exceptional virtual & F2F presentations – pitches, Town Halls and conference speeches.

He delivers practical keynotes for our new hybrid world in the core areas of presenting, selling & influencing, virtual & F2F:

- Exceptional presenting

- Effective client meetings

- Personal branding & differentiation

He coaches Global Chairs, EMEA Managing Partners and CEOs and has worked with clients such as Baker McKenzie, Simmons & Simmons, Carpmaels, Orrick, Burberry and Univar Solutions. He's been a teacher, sales manager and UK Head of Learning for L'Oréal and Pepsi.

He has written four business books, including *Brilliant Selling* (now in its third edition, with 80,000 copies sold and translated into 14 languages) and *The Leader's Guide to Presenting*, which was voted 2018 UK Business Book of the Year.

Jeremy is married to Susie, has three children and plays numerous sports, including pinball, golf and cricket.

✉ jeremy@jeremycassellcoaching.com

🌐 www.jeremycassellcoaching.com

in www.linkedin.com/in/jeremycassell

Thought Leadership – The More The Merrier!

MINDY GIBBINS-KLEIN

Who are the real thought leaders? Are they some exclusive group of rare individuals who are to be extolled and revered? Actually, there are many thought leaders and potential thought leaders out there in the business world, but we don't always hear from them or about them. Smart companies are recognising the value in having many thought leaders in the organisation, and they are reaping the benefits of this approach. If you run a business or are a leader in someone else's business, you may want to consider developing as many thought leaders as possible in your organisation. Let me explain why and exactly how to do it.

What thought leadership means today

Firstly, let me explain what I mean by thought leadership. It is having the courage to share big, bold, exciting, original ideas and content *and* being recognised by your industry for those ideas. That definition is meant to provide a framework of sorts, and it also allows for the subjective decisions about what is and what isn't big, bold, exciting or original.

As you can see, there are three distinct parts to this definition:

1. Developing the ideas.

2. Having the courage to share those ideas.

3. Being recognised by the influencers and your market (clients and prospective clients).

4. All three components need to be in place for thought leadership to thrive. Imagine what would happen if you had the idea development and the courage to share, but the recognition did not happen. To have thought leadership requires some thought *followership*.

Benefits for the leader

There are probably dozens of benefits to the individual leaders, and once you understand them, you will see why thought leadership is not only a good idea but essential for any forward-thinking organisation. Remember, this concept requires the organisation to go above and beyond the average in their market, and it is only the ones who truly care about the development of their leaders who will embrace it.

Fulfilment

My team members come alive when they share ideas that are accepted and implemented. They feel valued and valuable. They know that we are not interested only in their productivity and results but their ideas and opinions. Most organisations leave so much potential thought leadership completely untapped, but since this is an area we work in, we prioritise it.

Think of a time when you shared a big original idea and were recognised for it. I hope you can come up with at least one memory?! If not, you may want to reflect on the business you're currently involved in and the quality of the leaders around you…

So, what about you as a leader? Are you actively encouraging other leaders to step up and share their best ideas, both internally and externally? Remembering how that makes you feel can be really helpful, and it may remind you how you built your own career. It can take a little extra effort if you are creating a new focus on thought leadership, but just like anything important in life, it is well worth it when you achieve the result.

Career Development

I have worked in organisations and teams where career development and leadership development were high on the priorities list, and I have been part of other organisations where it wasn't even part of the vocabulary, much less the strategy. I'm sure you know which one felt better to me as a leader! The investment in me in terms of being able to express and share my best ideas led to deep loyalty and commitment.

If you allow team members to write and speak on behalf of the organisation, such as delivering presentations, writing articles and blog posts, recording podcasts and videos and engaging on social media as themselves, you are helping them build their personal brand while strengthening the company brand.

Of course, there is always the risk that if you let someone spread their wings and build their own brand or following, they could leave and join another organisation who has noticed their thought leadership, or they might want to start their own gig. However, I believe we need to trust, respect and invest in our people, and I think most people will appreciate that trust, respect and investment and repay you with the loyalty and commitment I mentioned earlier.

Benefits for the organisation

First of all, you get to share the workload of spreading thought leadership to your market (although it often does not feel like *work* when you are sharing exciting ideas, it still takes time to craft and distribute content).

Secondly, you can create more buzz with more people. Sometimes less is more, but this is one instance where more is more! Consider involving more people, even everyone at every level, to share the company's brand messages. Don't worry if you only have a small team. You can include supporters, partners, suppliers and even clients if you create the right strategy and environment. I have done this very successfully with all of my companies, and I have helped hundreds of clients to do it. I'm very happy to share the exact strategies that have been successful for us during the past two decades. Just find me, mention this chapter, and we will hop on a call.

You can also improve the retention in your team and organisation overall. It has been proven many times in employee satisfaction surveys and employee exit interviews that feeling like one is making a significant and important contribution is the factor that most directly influences that person's decision to stay or leave. So now we are talking about a tangible benefit: the bottom line.

Finally, you get to benefit from more diversity of thought and be seen for that diversity in your industry. One client I have been working with has made an extra effort to pull in as many different points of view and include as many different employees as possible to contribute to the company's brand as a thought leader.

How to develop thought leaders

There are many things that can be done to bake a thought leadership focus into the culture of the business. Below are my top four ideas.

1. Give people time and space to craft their best content and deliver it. The issue with most businesses is that people are asked to focus on their core job, and they are given objectives that take them right to the limit of their time, attention and energy. Thinking and creative time tends to be a nice-to-have once all the other essential tasks have been done. Which means it's often put on the back burner, and for many people, it never happens.

2. The increased pressure on team members, as a result of the pandemic and economic challenges, downsizing and the 'new normal' of work-from-home and hybrid work situations, means that for many people who remain in the team, there is even more work to do. Adding thought leadership objectives to an already full plate seems counterintuitive, but as I mentioned above, that is exactly what will keep people engaged and happy. Find a way to include these important but not necessarily urgent goals, and your organisation will reap the rewards in the long run.

3. Work with the line managers who know, at a deeper level, their team members' goals, skills,

interests and talents. If you run a sizeable organisation, chances are you are a few levels of management removed from many of your staff members. It would be impossible to intimately know more and more people while managing the overall business and strategy. This is why layers of management exist: to spread the work and give each employee a direct manager, and each manager a manageable number of direct reports.

Build this into the personal development plans for each employee and consider having a thought leadership element in assessments, bonuses and other means of compensation. Progressive and forward-thinking organisations are doing this already, and it is no surprise that many of them are on the 'best places to work' lists. As mentioned in point 1 above, this is a guaranteed way to ensure your people know they are valued for their ideas as well as their output.

4. Make it part of the overall communications strategy, then communicate it effectively internally as well as externally. Be ready to explain the strategic value to anyone who is reluctant to share their ideas, possibly because they were ignored in the past or simply are not in the habit of being part of the organisation's communications strategy. Publicising your mission will engender goodwill and positive attention from your market.

You could even make it part of your recruitment plan or PR strategy if you are fully behind this initiative.

Aiming higher: ThoughtFUL leadership

If you feel you and your business already do a good job in the area of thought leadership, why not aim for the next level: thoughtful leadership? Simply put, this is thought leadership content that has even more thought and more heart put into it, or Thought Leadership 2.0, as I like to call it.

Since I began writing and speaking about thought leadership in 2008, the term has grown in usage and popularity. Unfortunately, as is the way with popular or trendy topics, it has lost quite a lot of its original meaning, and as a result, has become quite commoditised. It sometimes seems like everyone and his dog is claiming to be a thought leader. Although I'm quite impressed with the thought-leading dogs (!), this dilution of the extra-special, truly original thinking has made it harder than ever for real thought leaders and their content to be seen and appreciated. Simply put, if everyone is a thought leader, then no one is.

True thought leadership has always been measured on results, which includes followers, fans, engagement, etc. That is the proof, as it were. These days, with more noise than ever, more books being published than ever, more podcasts, videos and basically more content than ever being thrown at us, the one constant is whether people engage or not and whether the market calls you a thought leader (don't even dream of calling *yourself* one!).

Have a higher standard

Organisations that commit to truly thoughtful leadership know that they cannot settle for mediocre content. They are also aware that quality is even more important than quantity, and this is reflected in all content associated with the brand. Producing a lot of content that doesn't say anything new, exciting or original is just adding to the noise.

But how can you tell if your content is truly exciting or original? You may think it is difficult to assess the quality of your own company's content, and you would be right. You may need an external point of view, guidance and direction. Feel free to get in touch with me anytime to discuss the options for creating a robust, thoughtful leadership strategy in your organisation.

Having read this far, you may be thinking that this all seems like a lot of work and a lot of effort. Yes, it is. And the good news is that thought leadership is a choice, and so is thoughtful leadership. Not every leader will aspire to lead with their thinking, and that is fine. Not every leader will be willing to put in the effort required or share communication opportunities more equitably throughout their organisation. They may be fearful of losing control or losing their best people. They may not understand the benefits to the organisation and to the individuals who are part of the team. They may simply not realise that society has become more inclusive and that keeping the responsibility of thoughtful leadership at the top echelons belongs to the last century.

If you see yourself as a truly thoughtful leader, you will be seeking opportunities to go above and beyond to develop yourself, your brand and your people. And you will win in this new era. Good luck and have fun!

Mindy Gibbins-Klein MBA FRSA FPSA is an international speaker and executive coach who turns leaders and experts into thought/ful leaders and published authors. She runs three multinational companies which have won and been shortlisted for 17 awards. Mindy has authored and co-authored 12 books, and her clients have written and published over 1000 books.

Over the past 25 years, Mindy has presented to and coached over 50,000 business executives and entrepreneurs in 18 countries. Her TEDx talk *Sometimes You Need to Change Yourself to Be Yourself* has nearly one million views. She has been featured over 100 times in the media, and her work has been licensed and syndicated across the globe.

A native New Yorker, Mindy currently resides near London in the UK with her long-suffering husband, who is secretly proud of her entrepreneurial spirit.

🌐 www.mindygk.com

🌐 www.bookmidwife.com

🌐 linktr.ee/mindygk

So You Think You Want To Be An Entrepreneur? Do This First

JON KEEL

To succeed as an entrepreneur, you must follow proven time-honoured principles of entrepreneurship. Being an entrepreneur is not for the fainthearted.

I share this from over 45 years of business experience, having owned four separate businesses and working with almost 1,300 clients in my consulting business over the past 24-plus years. I've made many mistakes and am sharing my insights and wisdom here to save you time, money and a lot of pain.

Why become an entrepreneur?

The truth is that we entrepreneurs are the key to a growing worldwide economy. It's certainly not large businesses, which we have seen over the past 20 years to be net job losers. As we entrepreneurs grow our businesses, we can hire more employees and become positive contributors to our local economies and communities.

We can offer the opportunity for our employees to grow personally, professionally and emotionally and have improved family lives. All these make our communities better places in which to live and contribute to society as a whole.

Along with this comes the opportunity to provide financial and emotional security for our families, not relying on a faceless organisation to do what is our personal responsibility. Added to this is the ability to make deep, long-term friendships, something I've personally experienced and continue to experience.

So yes, if it fits you and your dream, move forward with vigour.

Most would-be entrepreneurs shouldn't

Many entrepreneurs with whom I've worked with over the past almost 25 years began their business careers with an expertise, either from education or having worked in a particular job. At some point, they decided they'd prefer to be in their own business, be their own boss.

They don't understand that being a business owner is a totally different 'animal' from being an employee. There's no guarantee of a paycheck, for one. There's more risk when you own your business; your money and possibly more is on the line. Your commitment has to be one of 'all in'.

I recall my youngest daughter had the opportunity to buy an existing fitness franchise where she had worked part-time for several years. With my financial background, I evaluated the numbers. The opportunity looked good for her to double the revenue in a year, although I told her, 'Plan on working a minimum of 70 hours a week for the first several years.' Since she was my daughter, she knew about working hard, and she did.

She had an 'all in' commitment and doubled the revenue in a year. At the same time, she needed to negotiate her business commitment with her husband and two small children.

Many entrepreneurs I've known don't have this 'all in' commitment.

Do you? And is your family in it with you, willing to support you in your efforts?

Do you have the right mindset?

Business owner mindset is completely different from employee mindset.

As an employee, you work and get paid. As an entrepreneur, you work, work, work, and hopefully get paid. This will require mental toughness, perseverance, resilience, and more, particularly in the beginning stages of a business. It's more than just having a good idea. You have to be able to stick it out through the tough times, and they will come.

Witness what occurred in 2020 and into 2021 with the pandemic and shutdowns. I talked with many entrepreneurs who had never experienced anything like this. I'll admit that, although I went through the gas crisis of the 1970s, Y2K, 9/11, the 2008 recession and several other situations, I could never have predicted what happened. Obviously, no one could.

Times like this can cause you to doubt yourself, your dream of a successful business, and your own ability. Personally, my consulting business's new revenue basically dried up during this time; no new projects. Even after more than 20 years in business, it was tough. But this is where my mental toughness, perseverance, resilience and basic belief in myself came through.

I pivoted to start another related business as well as engage with people I knew who needed coaching. That made things a little better in 2020/21.

Are you mentally tough? Have you shown perseverance and resilience up to this point in your life?

These questions are important to realistically address and even get some outside perspective before you embark on your entrepreneurial journey.

There are additional mindsets on which you need to focus.

First, what's your emotional intelligence or maturity?

When disappointments occur (either self-inflicted or from outside situations), how do you handle them?

I believe Goleman's book on Emotional Intelligence is a required read for business owners.

I recently worked with an individual (minority partner) for about a year who had big emotional intelligence issues, which I didn't know going in. He had a complicated family situation to the point where he would disappear for several days at a time. 'It's just too much for me; I have to be by myself,' was his standard reply.

He perceived himself as a business owner; as is fairly obvious, he didn't possess the mindset to be an owner, nor had he read Goleman's book I had sent him, and I disengaged him from that particular business.

As an entrepreneur you have to work through it when 'crap' happens. Or, as a mentor once told me, 'Become a DWIT (do whatever it takes).'

The last mindset to have is delayed gratification. As business owners, we need to eliminate any 'microwave' quick results thinking. Starting and growing a successful business is a long term game. I've met no pure overnight successes in the entrepreneurial field.

Having this attitude moves us from 'transactional' thinking to 'relational' thinking. When we think transactionally, it's all about the next deal, the next sale. Relational thinking, on the other hand, allows us to see our business over the long term. We make decisions with that in mind.

I recall a recent situation with a former client where I (notice I said I, and not one of my employees) made a mistake that cost the client several thousand dollars. He didn't realise until we weren't working together anymore. He came back and asked me to write him a check for the mistake. Short term thinking would have been to say, 'Sorry, but no.' Because I've learned to have a long term view, I wrote him a check. Did I have to? No, it was just the right thing to do. And he's already referred several other clients to me. A good investment on my part.

That thinking comes from focusing on the relationship more than the transaction.

You must continually learn and grow

I remember thinking when I graduated from college (not a requirement to be an entrepreneur, by the way), my learning was over.

Not at all. My learning was just beginning. And as I had the opportunity to buy into my first business, I quickly began to see how little I really knew.

From that point over 40 years ago, I've had a continual hunger to learn more; on a vertical learning curve, so to speak.

This is a truth you must embrace. Develop the student mentality that there's always more you can learn and know. This is important professionally and personally.

A model I like is the Johari window, a quadrant (the four areas of the quadrant are known to self/known to others – the arena, known to self and not known to others – façade, not known to self but known to others – blind spot, and not known to self and not known to others – unknown). I use this in my planning and regular business evaluation.

I've become a prolific reader over the years. Rate yourself – how many books do you read annually, monthly, weekly?

The truth is you need to read more.

Two of my values that relate to this are growth – I continually get better at what I do and how I do it, and excellence – good enough doesn't cut it.

Only by continually learning will you grow. And as a mentor once told me, 'If you're not growing, you're dying.' By learning and growing, you'll be able to develop a sustainable competitive advantage; I've found that many business owners don't continually learn and grow. As the line from *Pretty Woman* goes, 'Big mistake, big, huge'.

What are your blind spots? What are your unknowns? By definition you don't know these, but you can keep asking questions, 'What do I need to know that I don't, and that is not known by others'? The answers will come if you keep asking the questions.

Some examples:

Finance – how well do you know the financial numbers that affect your business? You don't need an advanced degree, but a basic understanding of finance can keep you out of big problems down the road. It's not all profit and loss, by the way. You have to know how your cash flow is affected by business decisions you make. No cash, no business.

Marketing and Sales – these are two separate areas, both important. I've encountered literally hundreds of businesses over the years that were weak in both areas. You don't have to become an expert in both (although I suspect as a founding entrepreneur, you probably know how to sell).

It makes no difference how superior your product or service is if your target market doesn't know about it and if you don't know how to get an order. Again, no sales, no business.

In many cases, particularly when your revenue is less than several million annually, you may not have the time or expertise to do one or both of these functions. You still need a working knowledge, though, to be able to ask the right questions if you decide to intelligently outsource these areas.

Wellness – this may sound weird in an entrepreneurial book, but if the past several years of shutdowns have shown us anything, wellness is important, if not critical. Wellness includes more than mental health; physical and emotional health are also important.

Areas of wellness include self-talk, mindfulness, movement, nature, technology, gut health, validation and sleep.

For years I literally abused my body (physically, mentally, and emotionally) by my negative self-talk; zero to low mindfulness; very low body movement; not getting out in nature regularly; abuse and misuse of, or over-reliance on technology; not eating right; relying on external versus internal validation; and not getting enough sleep.

I plan to live many more years, taking the long term approach to my wellness. It does no one any good (myself included) if I make tons of money but am not mentally, physically, or emotionally healthy. I will say the same to you about yourself.

I began several years ago educating myself in these areas and changing my behaviours; as a result, my odds of living many more years have increased.

This is something you must also do if you want a truly successful life to go along with your successful business. As an entrepreneur, you have a number of people counting on you.

But wait, there's more!

I'll leave you with this. Congratulations on considering becoming an entrepreneur. It can sometimes be a lonely journey, although it needn't be. Your friends (and maybe even family) with jobs won't understand you. Don't try to explain.

Find other entrepreneurs you can trust. Having this kind of network will pay dividends.

And whatever you do, no matter how hard it gets, in the words of Winston Churchill, 'Never, never, never give up.' You owe it to yourself, your family, and your future generations to grow a successful business.

As George Gilder said of the entrepreneur, 'He casts aside his assurance of 40-hour weeks, leaves the safe cover of tenure and security, and charges across the perilous fields of change and opportunity. If he succeeds, his profits will come not from what he takes from his fellow citizens, but from the value they freely place on the gift of his imagination.'

Jon Keel has developed a reputation as a results-oriented Business Advisor, having been involved in this role since January 1997. In addition to being CEO and Founder of Improved Results, LLC, which he founded in 1997, he co-developed the Xavier University MBA E-Business program, where he taught Online Marketing and E-Commerce. He also founded Improved Together, LLC), a LinkedIn SaaS business in June 2020.

He frequently speaks to audiences about performance-based marketing for online and offline businesses. He has written several books, numerous articles and has appeared on several TV and radio news and talk programs. He co-developed the first pay-per-click search engine bid management software and wrote the first book on pay-per-click search engines, *Instant Web Site Traffic*.

To get his free report, *Entrepreneurship Basics*, go to www.ImprovedResults.com/basics

🌐 www.ImprovedResults.com

🌐 www.ImprovedTogether.com

Is Recruitment A Dirty Word?

NICK MARANGOS

Back in 1999, when I started on this amazing journey, sales recruitment was a very different industry from what it has become today, for a number of reasons. The aim of this chapter is to put my views on whether recruitment is considered a dirty word, and I would like to change the perception of the of recruitment industry for companies and for candidates to help everyone to find their best hire and new role with ease and as little stress as possible.

Using an agency

I believe it all starts with the decision that you are looking to hire or want to find your next career move. The experience when looking for a job, or looking to hire someone for your team or business, has more than likely not gone as smoothly as one would hope and has left you disappointed or with a negative experience. To keep it simple, there are two methods to recruiting talent into your business if you decide to use an agency – contingent or retained.

Let me explain the difference

Contingent is typically engaging with a number of agencies and agreeing terms and percentages with the fee based on the first year's annual salary with no financial reward until the candidate has accepted the role and a start date has been agreed. The invoice can be presented on the first day of employment for that individual. Alternatively, you can go down the retained route – where the company in question will engage one agency on an exclusive basis with a clear payment plan – a small deposit of 1/3 of the fee paid upfront, and the remainder paid once the role is filled and they have delivered.

I believe this is not common knowledge for many hiring managers, and so typically, they go down the contingent route. Also, it is much easier for the hiring manager to go down this route as they have less push back from the rest of the business in HR or Finance.

Over the years, I have spoken to a number of hiring managers and owners of businesses, and they have always felt that by giving me or one of my team a brief, and we have agreed terms – we are now engaged, and it's our duty to fill the vacancy with no financial commitment their side. No surprise – this approach leaves a number of unfilled roles with many frustrated recruiters and hiring managers. I believe this is where the industry suffers the most, as there is a lack of communication from both parties, which in turn slows the process to a virtual standstill. The candidates in the process are then let down and don't receive the right experience with the agency and their potential new employer. Sadly.

The truth is that not every leader or hiring manager understands the cost implication of getting it wrong, and the market is stuck in its ways with the mindset that recruitment agencies lower their standards, which has a knock-on effect.

As a candidate, I believe the experience is equally challenging finding an agency that understands what you do, and you can relate to them. Also, no money is exchanged at all during the enter process – so it's totally relying on the integrity of the consultant who has rung you from out of the blue after seeing your profile on LinkedIn or a job board. You typically have a few minutes to really come across to the agent, sell yourself to your best ability without knowing if there is a role or not, and answer some very personal questions that you need to reply to in order to be considered for a vacancy. I believe this is a much more challenging position, as you are exposing yourself to the unknown and have no guarantee of getting in front of the client or having an interview. The truth is – this does not need to happen, and this can be resolved in a very simple way.

I would like to use a case study that happened in 2020 during the pandemic. My client is a 50-person Software-as-a-Service company based in London and Dubai. The owner is the CEO, and he had just hired a Sales Director who had come from one of the bigger competitors, and he was told to go and hire two sales guys for the team without using an agency.

When we came across this client, we started a dialogue on what they were looking for, and discovered the Sales Director had interviewed over 23 candidates from agencies, and also many more who had applied directly over six months. None had been successful for a number of reasons, either in the wrong location, salary too high, or not the correct sales experience. This had taken valuable hours out of the management team while still not securing the right salesperson. This causes unnecessary stress and frustration. The business had the budget to hire through an agency, but didn't really know how to work with them.

My initial call with the Sales Director was to explain we only work on retained assignments and would ask for a small deposit as a commitment for them to stop using any other agency. We could map out the market for them, meaning we could look at their competitors and target the right salespeople who may be interested in a conversation.

You must take the time to brief and work with an expert agency to help you source the best talent, so that you can continue with your day job. The terms can be easily agreed upon with a split payment plan agreeable to both.

The truth is it takes the pain away from the client, and the candidate will have a better experience and be represented with the best intentions, with a salary they are willing to accept.

5 key principles

1. Choose the right agency – candidate and company.

2. Make sure you are fully briefed on what to expect in the process.

3. Good communication skills, and listening to both parties.

4. Good culture, and look after your staff.

5. Make sure you make the right offer, and help through to onboarding.

1. How do you choose the right agency?

As a hiring manager or business owner:

I believe you must do your research and make sure the agency has some experience in your market; you can ask for examples or case studies of what they have delivered and the timeframe it took to successfully complete.

Agree terms before any engagement commences, such as payment dates, rebate period with percentage and a schedule for delivery. Ideally, you have given this project/assignment to this agency exclusively (no other agent being used) or on a retained basis (deposit £).

In truth, the speed of feedback is crucial as slow communication will not give a good impression to the candidate and will allow them to have their head turned by other opportunities. With the technology available today, it can be a very quick turnaround for both parties.

For a candidate:

Same process – find an agency that is clear on their website and on social media that this is their area of expertise. Also, the consultant at the agency needs to be on a similar wavelength so that they represent you with the best intentions. Don't forget that these agents are working for you, but the client will hire the best candidate – so it's important to build rapport.

2. Fully briefed

We take pride at Mason & Wake to have a clear understanding of the job description – we have a detailed call with the hiring manager to discuss the role. This is to make sure that we can fully brief the candidates, and it also helps if we advise the client of any additional pointers and consult with them to manage the expectation. Clients will often ask our candidates at interview if the role is what they expected, and whether Mason & Wake gave the correct information.

3. Good Communication

I believe that the key to completing a painless placement comes down to honesty, transparency and regular communication. This will help the momentum, and there is an old saying, 'time kills deals'; in other words, any delay from either party can cause a problem. As an agent, it is imperative to keep close to the client and the candidate, and in truth, the salary has to be ironed out from start to finish. What they would accept and what the client can offer. There are many examples of us securing the right candidate for the role with our clients by flagging and regularly checking that this is what both would accept.

4. Good culture fit and looking after your staff

I believe that when you are looking for a new role with a new company, you need to be clear and confident that you are joining a business that you will be comfortable with and that is going to suit your personality, and that they have a similar outlook on work/life balance. Today with the change to much more flexibility with most organisations, the ability to be freer to choose your location of work and movement from home and the office is key. The benefits a company offers are equally important today. There are a number of additional perks available, such as gym membership or private health insurance, and this is a huge decision maker. Our role at Mason & Wake is to ensure this is clarified to the final detail to avoid any disappointment with either party.

5. Accepting the right offer for you

I believe this is an area where a strong agency will stand out for the company and the candidate in question – the attention to detail in reading the offer letter carefully and making sure you negotiate on anything you are not clear about or would like changed, such as probation period, number of days for annual leave, and when bonus or commission is paid.

The importance of having the agent relay any amendments without causing any alarm or delay in the acceptance of the role is key.

Resigning from your current employer is also very sensitive and has to be done in a professional manner with a clear message. Expect a counteroffer – many companies will try and offer an increase in salary and perhaps a promotion – but according to recruitment consultants Office Angels, 'Many would advise you to decline the counter-offer. According to the stats, up to 80% of those who accept counteroffers end up leaving their current employer within 6 months, and 9 out of 10 leave within a year.'

This is a delicate situation and needs to be handled with the utmost respect, so the agent should be there as a consultant, not a salesperson. I believe as a consultant you need to have very good listening skills and be able to put the emotions aside. This is why it's important to have a close relationship with the client from the start, and with the retained approach, this will take the pressure off the agency and allow a calmer and less salesy approach to closing the candidate for a decision.

Once the start date is agreed, it is very important to stay in touch until the individual has signed and has confirmed they have resigned. Things can still go wrong at the onboarding stage; other opportunities may arise, and personal circumstances may change – so making sure the candidate feels you are approachable and there for them is a must.

Recruitment is a fantastic industry job, and I am very fortunate to love what I do – simply in that I can facilitate a career move or pay rise and bring joy to their lives again. Technology cannot replace humans in this area, and that is here to stay.

Hope you have enjoyed reading this chapter, and please get in touch if you have any questions or would like to hear more.

Nick Marangos is on a mission to build a global sales search firm and turn recruitment into a respected industry. He has been in the sales recruitment industry for over 20 years, having started his career in Australia in 1999 in Sydney. He has managed to work across three continents, helping grow sales teams in a number of industries and at various levels of seniority.

He has never written anything on recruitment or any industry before but, since Covid, the business mindset has changed and there is an adjustment needed on how hiring for a sales team should be done. He has managed a number of sales recruiters in London and won contracts with several impressive organisations. His purpose and passion is to help businesses experience the most pain-free hiring process. In a nutshell – Nick is looking to educate those who have had bad or negative experiences when using a recruitment agency.

✉ nick.marangos@masowake.com

🌐 www.masonwake.com

in www.linkedin.com/in/nickmarangos/

Connecting To Your Future One Life At A Time

JAY MOORE

You must embrace the truth that your own brand value, and one of the most important assets you can provide others, is your network.

'It is not what you know, but who you know, that matters.'

In the mid-90s, I'd do a short workshop, 'Branding You: The Productisation of the Most Important Brand of Your Life', that I delivered mostly to the sports marketing department students at the University of Oregon. I had the students do an exercise to explore just what value the entire educational degree they were pursuing was going to add to their own human brand and its value to others. The outcome always startled a good number of students as we discovered that general education, subject matter expertise, physical fitness, communication skills, leadership and team-building skills, and emotional intelligence (a new concept then), all added up to about the same amount of brand value as your personal network of humans did.

A recent loss of a mentor and inspiration of mine illustrates just what a legacy you can create when you are open to proactively networking with those who you are supposed to be connecting to, one human at a time. Patrick Fallis was an ex-Imagineer who consulted for Disney on contract and would, in the same day, be driving a new innovative marketing launch strategy for *Pirates of the Caribbean* and, before the day was over, flying from LA to Redmond, WA, to rewrite the Exchange Server code so everyone at Disney could get back into their email.

His touch on my life was much deeper and much more profound.

We met at my first WWDC (Apple's World Wide Developers Conference) in 2004; he and his business partner, Stephen Crane, were in line at a coffee shop, and we struck up a conversation. Before the day was out, we'd begun our first of many discussions to rewrite the history of mankind. His impact on me was even more profound; I so miss random calls that ended up making my day and re-aligning me to my purpose. Out of habit, he'd introduce me to two or three people I 'needed to know' based on those conversations. I learned from him the powerful habit of daily taking time to connect those

I know need to meet each other in a karmic effort to impact the lives of others.

Network like the quality of your life depends on it

Being keenly aware of the impact of my network on the path my life might take and the impact I can provide others has always been at the core of my commitment to building a high impact network. More importantly, it should never be a means to an end or driven by an input that is only meant to create desired output. Giving first to others and being a source of value to those that are in your network is one of the most profound ways you can contribute value in life. My process is very simple; when I'm in conversation with a person I want to give to, I try to think of two or three people that I should introduce them to, and then each morning, I try to make those introductions. In the past, it has been primarily on email with a subject line like 'Two humans who should know each other, but I can't tell you why!' or 'Warning: The world may never be the same after you two connect'. When I say it used to be by email, it now happens wherever people are engaged and more often in LinkedIn Messenger, Telegram or WhatsApp by creating a group and making an introduction. The intention is always the same: to add value to others and to leverage your network of humans to others.

I speak at a number of events each year, and multiple times at each event, when I run into people I've known for years, they relate to me how an introduction made a deal, a company, and many times a lifelong friendship. While I don't ever try to track this, it does make it much easier to reach out to my network for introductions when I need to find the right human for a particular opportunity.

The network group that this amazing group of authors was recruited from – Business is Personal, or BIP – and my connection to it, is through Thomas Power, who I've always known to be one to two degrees away from all the top thought leaders and key industry contacts. I think of him as a human super-connector to superhumans, and I am inspired to learn from him as he helps network the world.

Two approaches learned: first, to be more intentional about thinking of introductions I should make, or discovering who I should reach out to, is more about tapping my intuition than just my ability to see logical patterns. I take time to get quiet, settle my thoughts, focus on the person or challenge that someone is having, and then let my subconscious surface the people who would be a good fit or should be engaged with a project or person.

My second and usually more random approach is to use LinkedIn and either do some subject matter searches or, while viewing new mutual connections between myself and others, trigger on who I know that I need to connect them with. The essential thing is to set aside time each day and at first set some intentions of how many introductions you'd like to make each week. I find if I can make two or three a day, it produces a very large impact, especially since some of those introductions involve hosting a Zoom or conference call.

Timing is Everything

One of the hardest lessons to learn is that sometimes the market timing is not right for a product, and perhaps the introduction or network connection might be early. I have three axioms:

1. Never wait to build a relationship.

2. Build your relationship around shared values.

3. Partnership is defined by a shared mutual interest in each other's success.

Those who can make the right introduction at the right time can be the magicians in creating an amazing new future. I know that when in an advisory role to a startup, sometimes there is understanding about what the organisation needs to learn next that makes it hard not to point out more of the learning they should do in other areas; but focus is everything, and thus that extends to the introductions and connections that are appropriate to the team as well. I remember one team where they *really* wanted to meet a particular personality, and I knew they needed to prepare for that. While I was able to get them closer, I had to warn my connection that they were still early, a little young and ambitious, and that their ideas were maturing quickly. It was one of those memorable high-profile introductions. They had the meeting; the team thought it went incredibly well, and later when I had drinks, my connection thanked me for having warned him about what stage they were at, and mentioned that he'd encouraged them to get things to a more mature state and to get back to him. After that, the team did a pivot, and they were at the right place to reach back out, and a deal was struck. When they reached out to thank me, the team had realised that they'd pushed too soon, and if it hadn't been for how I'd positioned them, they wouldn't have easily gotten a second look.

Sometimes we're not at the right place for a particular connection, but if we have the right attitude, we can grow into it. I find that if I use my intuition more and get very centred, I'm much more able to access the right humans that need to meet the other right humans, and timing seems to fall into place. Not every connection needs to be perfect, or even yield high results immediately, but alignment of goals, vision and mission always adds more alchemy to the introduction.

Celebrate Events to Connect Others.

I've been doing the ReConnect with The Jay Moore events for a couple of decades. It was all birthed out of the guilt I felt when I'd travel to a city and only be able to meet with a few of the humans I knew I'd been invited by, one of those sincere, 'Next time you are in Austin, SF,

LA, NY, Seattle, etc. let's do lunch or grab a drink'. So I began choosing one evening during a trip to organise a meetup at a venue that could hold 50–100 of my closest connections and my LinkedIn contacts, and then I'd send out an Eventbrite invite, organise with the venue (or find someplace that I didn't have to pay a reservation fee or space reserve fee). As I went throughout the country I'd have these ad hoc get-togethers, and it built a community around me as I always encouraged my connections to invite interesting humans and colleagues from diverse industries and backgrounds.

The success was nearly always amazing, near-family reunions before or after larger conferences. Others told me where to find the best business mixers they'd ever attended as I'd have musicians, C-suite, thought leaders, game developers, entrepreneurs, capital funds and just amazing people all diversely interested and who rarely crossed paths. The key is finding ways to create connections while you are doing something else, 'but the best relationships aren't the ones we've been planning'. Or like John Lennon said, 'Life is what happens to you while you're busy making other plans.'

I think we all try to reach out when we're going to events where we know a good many people. Always try to book multiple breakfasts and lunches and even dinners and drinks where you can have more intimate conversations with those you admire or are mentoring. Some of these had years-long traditions for me that were interrupted both by moving industries and by Covid.

I like to sponsor speaker dinners, networking events and especially 'after the after-party hospitality suites' in hotel venues near the conferences and events that I attend and speak at. This creates the expectation that if you can just get to Jay, you can get 'on the list', and the epic moments that have come from these events have so many stories and shared memories attached. Making moments and creating the times everyone talks about builds not only your role as a connector, but those who are extroverts and introverts that just like someone else making sure the room is filled with amazing and sometimes legendary people (by the way, it isn't because a person has large recognition or fame that makes them legendary). There is an art form to staging these types of events and gatherings, but suffice to say, sometimes no matter how much planning is done, things may not go to plan, and then the story becomes much more about the time that someone had to get bailed out of jail, or the repercussions when your noise complaint comes from the EVP of the largest global hotel conglomerate.

The key to being a super-connector is intention. I believe that you do it as a giving-first person without the desire to extract value from this. I understand for some agents that is the value they live on, but for most of us, if we make this part of our effort to add value to others, for me, this gives me such great joy when at least once, or ten times, at each event someone approaches me and shares a story of the amazing thing that happened with someone I don't even remember (in many cases) introducing them to. That reward can't be measured in monetary units.

Jay Moore is a massively parallel entrepreneur, human super-connector, blockchain pathfinder and industry insight merchant.

In his 30+ years in the video game industry, he has spoken internationally and is a domain expert on community branding, startup ecosystems, and new venture and strategic market planning. Jay has a successful track record in 12 new ventures, with four exits.

Most known for being GarageGames' marketing director & chief evangelist, he helped grow a community of 250,000 game developers. GarageGames licensed the first Triple A game engine for $100 and coined the term 'Indie Games', igniting the indie game movement.

Jay believes the future will be massively improved by blockchain, empowered by AI, and driven by an economy based on reaching our full human potential.

A known oenophile, his passion for new ventures is eclipsed by his love for his wife and that feeling of singularity when the sails are full, and the world has no limits.

linkedin.com/in/jdmoore

Twitter: @TheJayMoore

Telegram: @TheJayMoore

Mindset Principles
For Leaders

ANDREW MORGAN

In this chapter I am going to explore with you some key actions you can take as an entrepreneur that have served me well along the path of creating my future life. These actions are real-life ways that will put into practice three well-known mindset phrases that, if you haven't heard them yet, you are likely to hear in future. These are:

- Never Give Up

- Always Find a Way

- Do What Others Don't

Buzzwords and phrases such as these without action serve no purpose; in fact, they can become self-limiting over time if they are not accompanied by appropriate action.

We will find a way to put them to good work and assist you and your purpose well.

Two final points before we delve in:

1. Having a dream or a vision for your life and where you want to be at a certain time in the future is paramount. I have found that working on this and having it in place is not only priceless, it is also fun to do and brings clarity of purpose.

2. To help you achieve your dreams and vision, you need a plan of action that can point you in the right direction. At a top level, this is your business plan for one, three or five years, for example, and within it lies an action plan that you will follow to achieve certain milestones along the way.

Never give up

The truth is there will be times when you feel like throwing in the towel. Starting a business will offer up challenges that, although they seem familiar, will take on a different context for you. The reason for this – these challenges need to be overcome now in a very different environment. One where you have decided that the buck will stop on your desk.

Let that sink in for a moment. If you need to pick the phone up or scour the web for a solution to a problem, chances are you are going to have to pay for it. An administrative expense, a cost of a sale, whatever it may be, it will have repercussions for your bottom line profit when the accounts are due. If your former experience was as an employee, chances are there was someone who had the expertise within your organisation to solve these problems, or a quick business case would lead to a budget holder finding the additional expense to make the problem go away.

In your new world, an unforeseen issue occurring as a one-off situation may not cause you too much concern in your new venture. However, I have come to find over the years that these individual matters can build up into a larger feeling of concern and stress, and it is very easy to question one's resolve and determination. This is, of course, an excellent example of why a strong and detailed business plan can identify the path a venture is likely to take and therefore contain an accurate prediction of expected costs.

After 15 years in the corporate world, I finally made the decision I had been threatening to do a number of times previously. I heard myself saying to my boss the words that meant I wanted to give up my familiar way of life. Namely, work for a month, take home a salary, a bonus now and again, something that added up to perceived security for me at the time. Deep down though, I knew it wasn't enough, for a number of reasons particular to myself. If you have been in employment as well and are reading a book on entrepreneurship, you will have your own reasons too, which led to your own decision for your future.

The reason I recount this tale is because it led to a big change in the makeup of my friends and associates. When in the corporate world, 90% of my friends and acquaintances had very similar backgrounds to me in the world of the employee; they were concerned by similar problems to me – mortgage, car, pay rises and the like. I remember a couple of years or so later being quite astonished that my current circle of friends and acquaintances then were 90% self-employed business owners, concerned with business growth, local opportunities, growing their networks, government policies and so on.

The big realisation for me was that my former network was not equipped to support me in my new world. I didn't actively jettison friendships; I just gravitated towards these new groups of people. This is hugely important and a factor you must recognise on your journey as this support network will be vital to you, and I will expand on this in the next section.

Quite simply, there are people you don't yet know out there who will give you the confidence to never give up.

Always find a way

When a difficulty occurs, and you feel you don't have the expertise to solve it, you may have heard this sentence describing several ways of tackling this problem.

'Go over it, go under it, go around it or smash right through it!'

On the face of it, this may seem a bit trite; however, I know that this is a mantra that I needed to help me get past various difficult situations. The truth is that as an entrepreneur, you need certain strengths. Three of these are courage to face the unknown, belief that you have the solution within you, and the dedication to see it through.

At the start of my entrepreneurial journey, one of the most heartening things I quickly found out was that there are many people out there who want you to succeed, many people who are willing to share their knowledge and support you when you need it. This is where your human skills come to the fore, and you must find a circle of associates that is beneficial to your personal development and that of your business.

Talk to the right people, seek advice from sources that will give you clean, straightforward pointers gained from the type of journey that you are on. Be aware of the dangers of listening to those who are happy to tell you what they think and how you should act, but they have never been on your journey and may have other personal reasons for reinforcing their own image of themselves.

For me, I found this support within business networking groups in my early days as an entrepreneur. Just like building a sales pipeline, finding a team of people you can add to your close network takes time and commitment. If you do enough of it in the right places, you will build a strong network where in time, you will be contributing as much to the others as they bring to you. I still have, as close friends and associates, a number of people I met in my first year of business networking seventeen years ago, and it has been a joy to see their businesses progress and share the ups and downs of life with them. This comes from a common mindset and what it takes to achieve one's goals for yourself, your family and loved ones.

The mention of family and loved ones leads me to point out an important benefit that may not be immediately apparent at the start of your entrepreneurship journey. To never give up, to always find a way and, as we will touch on shortly, to do what others aren't prepared to do, are character traits that will become infectious. Those close to you will see these develop and will lean in towards you not only to support you but to catch some of this magic themselves. For a long time, I worked closely with my wife on one particular business, and our daughter, at a young age, captured these attitudes; they have helped her immensely as she has grown older and pays it back to me with continuing support and encouragement. That is a lovely position to find myself in, and I recommend it to others!

Do what others don't

When I look back at my early days in business, I now realise that at the time, I needed to change many aspects of my existing life. I have touched briefly on a couple of these above, namely developing a practical way to solve problems and finding the right mix of individuals. These are solved by interaction with others; for a moment, though, I want to focus on your inner resolve and what you are prepared to do for yourself and others. I believe this, amongst the many character traits needed to be successful in the entrepreneurial world, is way up at the top of the importance tree.

I knew that at a certain time in my business, I needed to apply a massive boost to raise the volume of sales to a higher level. Once that level was achieved, a new baseline would be in place, and further advancements would follow. This is where I needed to work longer and smarter for a relatively short space of time.

Let's take working longer first. At 6pm, I would find myself standing on the London-bound platform of my local station. An evening meeting was beckoning, and I was already tired after a breakfast meeting, a lunch meeting and commitments in between. It would have been very easy to think, 'No, it's OK, I'll go to the meeting next month'. I knew very well, though, that by not being there, I may miss meeting a person of significance, possibly not for immediate business, but equally important, a person with influence who would open doors I couldn't on my own.

And working smarter. It is very easy to stay within your own comfort zone, resulting in staying within familiar places with a crowd that you know well. Now, this is a cosy place to be but will not bring personal growth. Summoning a little courage and effort to knock on the metaphorical door of people you don't yet know can seem a little daunting. Again, refer back to the size of your dream and what you are prepared to do. The truth is you are only a newcomer on the first occasion; the second time you meet these people you will be well prepared and will understand their expectations of you a little better.

People will always remember what you did for them, too. As well as pushing yourself for your own development, think about how you can help others far more than they would expect. After a short while, you will become known as someone who is helpful and a pleasure to be around. This result can be achieved simply by listening to others, pointing them in a relevant direction, or being willing to meet up for an hour when their need is there. The outcome of this may not be seen for a long time, possibly even many years in the future. However, something you did, an act of care for another entrepreneur which you may even have forgotten about, will be repaid by a chance happening or a predetermined action. One of the reasons I am able to write this chapter is because many years ago, I made the acquaintance of new people in my life, happily went out of my way to be helpful, and a decade later, they reappeared with a new opportunity to connect and grow. Relationships take a long time to nurture, but the benefits are multiple.

In conclusion

Holding these mindset principles close to your heart will benefit your entrepreneurial journey as well as those around you in your life already. If you visualise for a moment a person you know whom you admire and aspire to be like yourself, then the chances are that person knows to never give up, has always found a way and will do that bit more than others to achieve their goals.

Andrew Morgan Having been in the entrepreneurial world since 2003, Andrew Morgan has built businesses in both event management and product sales. He has enjoyed the experience of self-employment and the opportunity to live his life by his calendar and not that of others.

One aspect of Andrew's experience that he has found particularly valuable is the wonderful diversity of people he has met over his years in business. He believes that mixing with individuals who possess varying talents and hail from a multitude of backgrounds helps enormously in achieving both business and personal success.

Although originally from the most northerly of English counties, Northumberland, he now lives with his family close to London in the county of Essex. Andrew enjoys the opportunity to travel around the UK for both business and leisure as for him, it always delivers wonderful surprises and experiences wherever one is prepared to look.

in www.linkedin.com/in/andrew1morgan

Your Company Is Now A Tech Company

CHRIS O'HARE

We are in an unprecedented time when incumbent companies are fast becoming obsolete through rapid disruption by faster moving startups with technology superpowers. These companies are fighting to adapt to the new whilst bringing along the baggage of the old ways of doing things and taking years to turn in the change in the face of a generational obstacle.

What we must identify is that technology has been creeping up on us for years and what would have been considered tech at the dawn of the 2000s is now a part of everyday life for many people.

Therefore, this is why many senior leaders around the world think that the future of all companies will be driven by software development. We will dive into why this has come about and how you can start to strategically think like a tech company.

The forever moving competitive advantage

The technological era started at the industrial revolution when manufacturing and technology combined to accelerate the growth of the world's economy. Never before have we seen production at this scale to create products faster, better, and cheaper. It's every individual's pursuit to be remarkable in today's world and, ultimately, better than their competition.

Fast forward to the modern-day, manufacturing has diversified into many different market sectors, which technology has enabled, further enhanced, or even produced its own sector by servicing the tech needs of other sectors. But something different was happening; we had moved into a new era where technology had separated software from hardware and was solely the manufacturing of software, spoken about in engineering terms but all virtual.

Software was becoming a tool that businesses didn't only leverage to do their day-to-day administrative tasks, but actually started using to create their own innovations – either to service their own needs by increasing efficiency, or to serve the needs of their customers but ultimately to ensure they had the bigger competitive advantage.

Now this distinction between software and technology is very important. Bill Gates said, 'Software is a great combination between artistry and engineering. Technology is just a tool.'

The tech giants of today are predominantly software companies; that's where they have made their vast wealth. Facebook started with a social network website, Google started with a search engine website and Netflix with a video streaming website – all of which are internet-based softwares, and all are virtual. But how have they got there? Well, the idea that their companies can scale and affect billions of people around the world at the same time with the touch of a button is very compelling.

Tech entrepreneur Marc Andreessen said, 'Software is also eating much of the value chain of industries that are widely viewed as primarily existing in the physical world. In today's cars, software runs the engines, controls safety features, entertains passengers, guides drivers to destinations and connects each car to mobile, satellite and GPS networks.'

With this logic, you can see that companies are leaning on software for so many parts of their business and would look unrecognisable without it. With this point in mind, software becomes so seamlessly integrated with a company that it blurs the line between the two.

Microsoft CEO Satya Nadella said, 'I think a lot about what happens in computing. It is getting embedded in our world. Computing is a core part of every industry. A car is now a computer. Software skills are a valuable resource. I don't think in ten years we will have these demarcations. We won't have the tech industry and other industries.'

Take FedEx, for example; from outside appearances they are just a delivery company, but if you take a closer look, they have an app, they have a smart website to manage parcels, they need to use software to manage logistics of the delivery of their parcels in an efficient way – all things they need to stay relevant in the face of competition. Are they a tech company?

When we look back at our own companies, you'll see that we are encroaching on this mentality. We have software for almost all of our business operations, some of which requires extensive technical skill to operate. We have smart products that integrate with apps, and dashboards telling us about how we use these products or how to get the most out of them.

Before long, you'll need to create smart products of your own to stay relevant in the face of stiff competition from the existing competitors, but also new market disruptors. With this, you'll need the skills of a software developer to create such a product, which requires ongoing maintenance and new features to keep up with your competition.

But software doesn't stop there; employees can be re-tasked if their day-to-day tasks are fulfilled by automation, often quicker than their human counterparts, as software can complete tasks concurrently, enabling you to scale your company without any extra payroll expenditure.

Software that can write itself

If you were told that software could write itself to ensure it's the most efficient it could be, and forever improve without the human limitations of sleep, food, and brain speed – isn't that the biggest competitive advantage we would see in all of human history? How disruptive do you think that would be?

This is what we are on the precipice of; before software creates breakthrough after breakthrough at a rapidly accelerating pace without the limitation of earthly problems. You've heard of this software: Artificial Intelligence.

The stuff of sci-fi comic books, futuristic predictions or how stereotypical robots will enable us to do our domestic chores. The thing is, Artificial Intelligence is already here and already disrupting humanity in very disturbing ways.

Facebook is already the most impactful purveyor of Artificial Intelligence. The way it uses its algorithms to create feedback loops forever, showing billions of users what it thinks they should see in order to create addicted eyeballs, essentially creating more advertising dollars for the shareholders. But this can have a dark turn when that user starts to become radicalised because each and every image, video, post, pushes them further into that way of thinking. This is why the United States, the birthplace of Facebook, seems so polarised between left and right to an almost vigilante war footing.

Let me reiterate – Artificial Intelligence is very powerful. Futurist and Tech Entrepreneur Thomas Power said, 'The machines will eat us; we will become one with the machine.' And as evocative as that may sound, he's right.

If you're not using this technology, then who might be? Your competition. The thing with Artificial Intelligence is that it requires a lot of data. Data that needs to be pulled in from various data sources to make sure it provides information that you can use. This data is your superpower; it enables you to quickly identify what is happening and adapt to changing requirements as they're happening. Artificial Intelligence can then start creating predictions for you.

For example, let's take a retail store. If they can draw data from real-time market data, news, social media and even your competitors, they may be able to see what is happening to either change a product line, create marketing to jump on a hype, or reduce exposure before submitting a purchase order. Then imagine Artificial Intelligence being able to see patterns within that data, and when those patterns appear again, an alert is triggered so you can react even more quickly. All the while, the prediction is getting more and more accurate with each gigabyte of data being consumed.

With the example, you can see the power of such a technology enabling them to see the unseen, giving the retail store a lead on the market and an unfair advantage which would ultimately contribute to healthier profits and growth.

Generation Zoomer

A strange thing happened; the advent of cheaply accessible technology made us addicted to our devices. The millennial generation created this technology, but young people known as Generation Z consumed it throughout their childhood as if it was a staple. This has had an irreversible impact on their behaviours.

But you may be thinking, 'Why is this important to my company?' Well, Gen Z's, or colloquially known as Zoomers, are your customers and employees of the future; we need to take into consideration what they want if you want to stay relevant, and you can guess a lot of what they want is tech-focused.

Attention span and patience are certainly lower than that of previous generations, wanting things almost immediately, the idea of waiting on the phone for customer support or even several days for a delivery is a no-go. This, along with their independent streak, means they turn to tech to either seek out the solution themselves or are immediately turned off.

As your future customers, you need to provide them with ways to solve problems themselves, detailed help, videos, and access to support chat. The rise of self-checkouts is evidence of their growing influence on society. Convenience over brands is the byword of this generation. This extends into the way they get shopping advice, which is a much more collaborative affair, taking recommendations from friends and social media influencers who are seen as more 'real' and trustworthy compared to traditional TV-born celebrities. This gives them an almost risk-averse vibe. They value tech-enabled products, great looking user interfaces and clever functionality that provides an all-round pleasant experience. They will pay more for a great user experience over product functionality.

One study found that 59% of Zoomers would only stay in a job for less than two years as an employee. They need to feel valued, work towards a greater purpose, but most importantly, they need to be given the tools to get the job done and do it well. Ninety-one per cent of Zoomers say company technology would influence their decision to take employment over rivals. This makes sense when their everyday life is so focused on technology that anything else would feel alien to them.

It's no surprise that the rapid growth of disruptive tech, including social media, convenience tech and, most recently, blockchain, has been so closely aligned with the rising age of Zoomers. We should sit up and take note of the changing landscape that Zoomers are creating.

Becoming a tech company

With all the points made above, you can see that the future is very much tied to technology or, more specifically, software. Can you afford not to be able to keep up with the overwhelming trend? Therefore, my suggestion is that you should treat your company as a tech company. Silicon Valley has dominated the markets, news and even your daily life for a reason. Software is the future.

To ensure you keep your competitive advantage, adopt Artificial Intelligence, and serve the upcoming Generation Zoomers, you need to make sure that software is a core driver of your company's digital strategy.

It may feel that the advantages are in favour of new tech-literate startups with no baggage to deal with, but you have something they don't, and that's customers. You know what your customers want and need. Adopt a digital-led culture within your company, expose your leadership team to technology ideas through experts. It is often then advantageous to build an education programme around these topics for key company team members; this will enable them to identify internal opportunities where technology could be a game-changer.

Some companies go as far as creating an innovation skunkworks within their company to enable research and development to be siloed from the 'mainstream' thinking of the rest of the company. This is a key problem when 'commercial' work needs to be done; innovation is ultimately the first to suffer.

Often the CEO and the senior leadership team are the bottleneck with their limited time; therefore, add someone to spearhead this new direction on your behalf. A Chief Technology Officer will help build out the technical elements of your grander vision and enable you to continue to be competitive into the future.

You are a tech company; welcome to the new era.

Chris O'Hare is the founder of Hare Digital, a Digital Strategy and App Development agency that has worked with numerous brands, including Royal Mail, BMW and the University of Sussex.

Hare Digital provides a Chief Technology Officer (CTO) for hire service alongside building complex web applications, mobile applications, workflow automation and emerging technologies, including the internet of things, blockchain and artificial intelligence.

Chris is a 10+ year developer and has a Bachelors and Masters in Computer Science with Business from the University of Sussex, where he has a First Class and a Distinction, respectively, along with multiple awards for his achievements and business from the university, and the city's business awards.

Chris's ability to translate technical jargon and problems into understandable concepts before applying them to business models relevant to the audience has been noted by several business leaders.

🌐 www.hare.digital/your-company-is-now-a-tech-company

🌐 www.hare.digital/podcast

🌐 www.hare.digital/social

Investing With The Best Entrepreneurs

OWEN O'MALLEY

Have you ever thought about becoming an entrepreneur? If so, you would aim to be a successful one. A simple definition of a *successful entrepreneur* would be, 'A person who finds a customer, sells them a product and does this many times over'.

While making the decision to leave my day job and become self-employed, I thoroughly studied my options. I researched the small- to medium-sized business statistics, and in light of the facts, I quickly realised that it was much better to invest in the best businesses in the world than to start your own business.

Let me share with you my findings and experience when comparing starting a business versus investing with the best entrepreneurs on the planet, so you can make an informed decision on the best course of action for your entrepreneurial life.

According to Embroker[1]:

- 80% of startup businesses fail in the first five years

- 90% of startup businesses fail after ten years

- 90% of businesses fail to achieve a total combined sales of one million and attain an average net profit of 5%

If you do the maths, here was my conclusion at that time: if you manage to beat the odds and become part of the 10% of businesses that survive, and get to the magic one million in sales with an average net profit of 5%, then you make £50,000. However, if you are already on a per annum salary after tax of £50,000, it does not make sense to start a business.

Some might say that if you build a business and sell it, then it will be worth all the extra effort. With a business turnover of one million and a net profit of 50,000, you will realistically only get offered somewhere between three to five times profit (which is 150,000 to 250,000) to sell your business. The proceeds from selling your business will only fund your lifestyle for the next three to five years,

---

1   https://www.embroker.com/blog/startup-statistics/

and then… you would need to start a new business again when or before you run out of cash.

Let us dig deeper into the 'facts of life' when starting up and running a business.

Embroker shows the following data:

- Approximately one third of new companies remain profitable

- One third of new companies remain at breakeven

- One third of new companies continue to lose money

Smallbiztrends[2] notes:

'If you want to start your business, don't let the startup statistics above put you off. After all, you're more likely to succeed if you've failed than if you've never tried. Consider, founders of a previously successful business have a 30 per cent chance of success with their next venture; founders who have failed at a prior business have a 20 per cent chance of succeeding versus an 18 per cent chance of success for first time entrepreneurs.'

---

2   https://smallbiztrends.com/2019/03/startup-statistics-small-business

Shares

How about investing in the best companies in the world, run by the best, talented people in the world? As you have seen from the startup statistics, it is tough to start and survive in business. It is even tougher to become qualified for and live with the intense scrutiny as a publicly traded company. The only difference between you and the CEO or founder of some of the greatest businesses in the world, if you invest in them, is the number of shares that you own compared to them. When you think about it, when you buy shares of a company, the CEO and all the employees are working for you!

The number one responsibility of a CEO and all the workers of a company is to increase shareholder value. That being the case, when you own shares in a large publicly traded company that employs thousands of workers all over the world in different time zones, they are all working for you to increase your shareholder value 24/7, even while you sleep in your bed.

The big challenge for you is to know how to pick the best publicly traded companies in the world to invest in to maximise your increase in shareholder value.

This is where we come in: for over 20 years, we have been working with individuals in 50 countries in 15 different languages, helping them learn how to choose the strongest publicly traded companies in the world to invest in. Another skill set that we pass onto our students is how to recognise when the greatest publicly traded companies in the world are also great value to invest in.

Robert Kiyosaki famously wrote in his popular book *Rich Dad, Poor Dad* that 'an asset − like a share that you invest in − is not an asset unless it provides you with an income'. This is the most important skill set that we teach our students: to be able to effectively 'rent' their shares and generate a monthly income from their portfolio of publicly traded shares.

You might say, 'How can you "rent" your shares to generate a monthly income? It sounds complicated! And… I have never heard of renting shares!' I, maybe like you, had never heard of 'renting shares' until I attended a Tony Robbins' Wealth Mastery Seminar in Hawaii, in March of 1996. Let me explain how the 'rent' works for shares.

The US stock share trading market, called New York Stock Exchange (NYSE), was first established in New York in 1792. Then came the NASDAQ market, opened down at Times Square, New York, in 1971. Then, in 1973, a very significant event happened in Chicago, when the options market was opened to give ordinary people like you and me the tremendous opportunity to trade options on publicly traded shares.

At the time of writing this chapter, only 10% of publicly traded companies in the world trade options were traded in the US options market, which means that from the approximately 40,000 publicly traded global companies, only 4,000 of them trade options in the US.

We use options to 'rent' our **NYSE** and **NASDAQ** shares in the Chicago Board of Options Exchange (Cboe[3]). There are two types of options that we can use to generate income from our portfolio of shares: call options and put options.

Call options

If you own a share that does trade in options, you can give the market the option to 'call your shares away' from you in the future. When you sell a call option, you agree to keep your shares during a fixed period and to allow the market to call them away from you at a fixed price, and for that service, you receive a payment called 'premium'. Here's what these terms mean:

- **Fixed period:** monthly options that expire the third Friday of every month unless this day is a holiday, such as Good Friday. In this rare case, such as 15 April 2022, the expiration day was Thursday, 14 April. Some companies also offer weekly options, which will expire on Fridays other than the third Friday of the month.

- **Fixed price or 'strike':** the agreed price at which the shares can be called away from you.

---

3   https://www.cboe.com

- **Premium, call income or 'rent':** the payment you will receive up front, when you agree to sell your shares at a fixed price in the future. You are, in effect, being paid to sell your shares in the future.

Shares that trade options must be bought in batches of 100 to be able to collect option income on them. One hundred shares of a company equals one option contract in the options market. If you only buy 99 shares, you are not able to collect call option income on those shares until you add one more share to your purchase. For example, you can buy 100 shares today for $10 per share in either the NYSE or NASDAQ share market. Then you can sell one option contract to agree to sell those shares back to the market at $11 per share in the future and get paid $0.50 per share today. This is an income of $0.50 on a $10 investment which is 5% 'rental' call option income.

Now that you have entered into this call option agreement, you are unable to sell your shares since they already have a pre-agreed option contract in place to sell in the future. This is like having tenants in your house, occupying your house while paying you a rental income to do so for a pre-agreed time period. If in the future, those shares are called away from you at the pre-agreed sale price of $11 per share, you will make a profit of $1 per share from the sale of the shares. This is a profit of 10% as you bought the shares for $10 and sold them (the shares were called away from you by the market) for $1 profit, which is a

10% profit margin. If you do the maths, you made an income of $0.50 (5%) to 'rent' the shares and a profit of $1 (10%) to sell the shares, totalling $1.50 (15%) profit.

Put options

The opposite of a call option is a put option. If you sell a put option, you are giving the market the opportunity to put the shares to you at a pre-agreed fixed price (known as the strike price) within an agreed time frame. If the market puts the shares to you, that means you are buying them.

In the case of put options, we also have:

- An expiration time, the third Friday of the month for monthly options

- A strike price, agreed price that the shares can be put to you

- A premium, or 'rent', which is the payment received to allow the market to sell you the shares

Therefore, selling put options instead of buying shares up front is a handy way to get paid up front to agree to buy a share that you are happy to own in the future. Effectively, we are buying shares… at a discount! For example, if a share is trading at $9 today and you would be very happy to own the share for a long term buy and hold position in your account, you can get paid $1.50 today to agree to buy the share for $10 in the future and make a 15% income up front, and a 5% discounted cost to buy in the future. As it has been quoted by Warren Buffett's fans, 'Sometimes, you can get paid today to buy shares you would like to own in the future.'

Compound interest

The last thing that we want to talk to you about is the concept of compound interest as a powerful tool to create long term wealth for you in the markets. As an example, let's consider dividend payments. What is this? Some companies divide and distribute some of their profit to their shareholders on a quarterly, bi-annual or annual basis. This is known as a 'dividend payment'.

When you use your dividend income to buy more shares, and when those new shares produce a dividend, you are now creating dividend income from dividend income. This making profits on profits is what compound interest is. We do the same with our call and put income in that we use this income to buy more shares which, in turn, provides more income. We are making option income from option income, which is a very, very powerful compound interest tool.

How powerful is compound interest to help you become financially free? If you do the maths on a model of investing 200 per month for 20 years at 2% monthly growth, thanks to the power of compound interest, in 20 years, your wealth will have grown to over one million. Likewise, if you invest 400 per month for ten years at 4% monthly compounded growth, you will reach over one million.

This is the power of compound interest (interest on interest).

In conclusion, the returns that you can get from the publicly traded markets are far more powerful than you can get from 99% of startup businesses. You can either work really hard to beat the odds and become part of the 1% of companies that become mega-successful, or simply invest in the best businesses in the world. The choice is yours to make, and we wish you the very best of luck in what you do in the future.

Owen O'Malley is on a 30-year mission is to create one million millionaires using the powerful global stock market as a vehicle to do this. He has already initiated over 1,000 investment clubs in 52 different countries. He has educated over 25,000 people in 15 different languages.

He has written and self-published seven books to date and has spoken at large global events with over 3,000 attendees. He has been interviewed on national radio and television stations. Owen has built a powerful team of educators and traders that can teach you to make your money work very hard for you.

Owen and his team have also empowered teenagers in the classroom to understand how the global stock markets work. His purpose and passion is to bring financial literacy skills to this and future generations to come. In a nutshell, Owen can help demystify the market for you.

🌐 www.ticn.ie/books

Improve Your Business Valuation Strategically From Day One

STEVE SANDERS

Start with the end in mind. Knowing the centre of gravity that hypothetically is where you'd aim to be acquired, or ready to be mainstreamed, or to reach maximum scale. Find your D-factors (desirability, disruption and defining factor).

Right away I want you and I to agree on two fundamentals: how humans need 'boxes'; and being clear about 'value'.

Give me a box

> 'With a box, I'll feel safe; unbounded ideas could end in chaos.'

All people seek boxes for ideas, metaphorically speaking. It helps us feel informed enough to make decisions. Without 'boxes', ideas end up unbounded; create uncertainty; cause discomfort.

You have a box around the value of your business. You seek boxes in which you fit your perception – why people value what you do. We are evolved as simple creatures who seek ways to simplify layers of complexities in an alien, modern world.

Perhaps your box is defined by product, service, or skills and experience. That's useful; it simplifies communicating, planning, selling, and delivering. When it comes to building a destination, achieving maximum value, this limits one's thinking as a leader.

First, figure out your impact, not features or capabilities

Product or service doesn't create value or benefit. You don't realise a benefit or value; your customer does, in their world. Consider what you emphasise, so it's well-received. Be precise in your thinking and how you communicate.

Features, advantages, capabilities and differentiation only convey as beneficial when pinpointing where customers gain value. Once you know the difference you make, that is what you amplify, and the greater your unique *desirability factor* becomes.

Imagine all ecosystem participants, the whole value chain, and those of your customers. Somewhere you will see a black hole of maximum gravitational pull.

I believe, in most cases, maximum growth comes from combining direct selling with an interlock into a vessel for growth.

A larger ecosystem player could hunger to possess your differentiation or dynamic capability, to reduce costs, heal a vulnerability, or differentiate themselves in their value chain. They could partner with you, sell for you, or acquire you. In doing so, potentially, they multiply their own valuation.

Whatever they choose, this alignment could become your black hole of maximum gravity, improving investor attractiveness or acquisition or mainstreaming options.

If you wish to exit via acquisition and don't have that level of attractiveness, you'll fetch a sub-optimal valuation. Perhaps they gobble up your revenue into theirs. With forethought and strategy comes greater valuation opportunity.

Define where your impact is greatest across value chains. Imagine a world where every customer solution in your market and related value chains includes your products or services.

Your challenge is to consider the triggers you can activate to cause the ecosystem to embrace you as its preferred norm. That is a mouthful, I know. As a concept, it is vital for you to grasp. By knowing the point of maximum gravitational pull, and maximum impact, therein could lie your *disruption factor*.

Decide where your idea can best be mainstreamed; it's almost certainly not by you. Barring rare cases, instigators of valued or disruptive capabilities rarely mainstream or reach maximum potential themselves. Critical mass to achieve this is normally held too firmly by larger players.

It's also no surprise that the biggest players in ecosystems, or entering from adjacent spaces, usually aren't effective at creating and proving such new capabilities. Their models, technology and people focus on efficiency at scale and struggle to enable 'intrapreneurship'.

There is a symbiotic relationship. Large players watch for best available new ideas or capabilities they can leverage, preferring those that already dovetail into their model for scaling. They're not buying your product; they're investing in your business for the *value multiplier* you can achieve.

By attractiveness, I don't mean how attractive your product is to customers. I mean, how attractive your business is to an investor, channel, or a partner; the level of advantage and simplicity for them to integrate into their business.

It follows you need to prepare now with that end in mind, do an alignment check, plot out gaps and course-correct.

Start fine-tuning your business, ready to grow valuation maximally.

Those with the highest valuations, or securing go to market alliances, designed into their fabric an attractiveness and ease of integration, often starting with that end in mind at the origination of their business journey.

The conundrum of mainstreaming or securing maximum opportunity

Selling what you do into a network that knows you, that's a good start. Single-minded pursuit of that will be part of success. Being preoccupied in that limited approach may cause you grief, revenue to taper off, or an inability to replicate.

Confront that reality, don't sit with pride atop the mound of small achievements, and don't be defensive. If you feel comfortable, therein lies a trap. Look over the next horizons, chart pathways, course correct. It is a journey, and so act upon that.

To mainstream or to prepare maximal opportunity, ideally at the time of origination, you'd challenge yourself relentlessly for proof of how it will be achieved.

Get it right, and an ecosystem finds you compelling, even inevitable. This must be pushed under the noses of those who have control, the channel that activates adoption.

Thus, you gain access to the value chain where your innovations make the most impact.

Tell me your principles, values, and purpose, and I'll decide if I want to work with you.

The idea of a 'defining factor' is included here not as an after-thought, but because of a trend that will affect most businesses in the coming 10–15 years.

Gen-X, Millennials to Gen-Z are disproportionately comparing themselves with your principles, values, and purpose before deciding who they will work for or buy from. As soon as better aligned alternatives exist, roughly 70% of them will shift. In ten years, that segment will be aged 20 to 50. That represents the most powerful consumer segment and the most attractive employees. The ramifications on your future are enormous.

You want to attract the best new talent, whose motivation will stem from passion, not only profit, to protect against customers abandoning you from their 'basket'. Investors value more highly principles-led businesses that clearly state their purpose and impact on the world. The majority of investors, buying power and talent will be swayed by these factors.

Decide on which impact, principles and values create your *defining factor*.

Use strategy best practices mindfully

Doing this will help you to ask better questions. Ask not what you can become in this horizon, but what you enable others to become in future horizons.

Amplify the importance of strategic analysis. Structured strategic thinking need not be convoluted or tedious. I guest lecture for the Warwick Business School MBA on bringing strategy frameworks to life using real founder-led client case studies. There, I experienced simplified real-world success from strategy frameworks, identifying where executives made harmful snap judgments, conversely contributing impact previously unforeseen by founders.

In less than 90 minutes, teams gathered around a couple of strategic models had added massive strategic value. I won't go on at length here, but it is worth looking into Porter's '5 Forces' and 'Value Chain', my simple 'Five Horizons Model', and combining with the Strategy Diamond from Hambrick and Fredrickson.

It is remarkable how business leaders carry on making sweeping assumptions and generalisations. These rudimentary filters challenge us and safeguard the future. Self-reflection is core to the most successful people. The same is true for the most successful businesses.

It's not about the value you enable, but how you can be even more valuable in someone else's hands in a future horizon.

You may know perfectly well how to sell your way to revenue and profitability. Adapting the context for your business across future time horizons, you will pinpoint greater value opportunity.

I spoke with a founder who was assured of his next growth sprint: seven million revenues to ten, in his 12-month 'Horizon 1'. He felt prepared to then reach 30 million in his 12-to-36-month 'Horizon 2'. Then he plans to exit. An investor may take control for months 30-to-54 'Horizon 3' and 48-to-72 'Horizon 4'.

Applying this horizons perspective altered his sense of reality. His aspiration for the valuation of his business changed. That took one challenge and three discussion points:

'Will your acquirer be buying your revenue, products, and channel reseller list, or will they be buying something of lasting value they can leverage in their value chain to achieve an acceleration or multiplier effect into their core portfolio?

If you sell your company to them for your product agencies, revenue, and customer or channel reseller list, you can expect only a modest valuation multiple.

Provide a dynamic differentiating capability that you know they'll value as it accelerates or has multiplier effects on their core business, then you can achieve a far higher scale of valuation multiple.'

I had his attention. Do I have your attention? I should.

Transition from manager to leader

Transition from being a 'manager in coping with the company processes' to becoming a 'leader in creating the future of the business'.

Assume for now that you know the contexts where you will in future become most valued. You also know where your ecosystem black hole of maximum gravity exists for you, perhaps a player that values owning you or partnering. Become an expert at pitching the 'why and how', and you will become most valuable to them.

You might not exit; you might prefer to retain control of a more lucrative future version of your business. Detach yourself from that future business as though you were an investor, acquirer, partner, or a channel. Visualise your new greater opportunity for your future self; tap the gravitational pull required.

Set up systematically for success

Doing this enables you to be scalable and impact growth without key persons being there in your unknown future of scaling.

When asked if a business is scalable by design, storytelling becomes very creative. Many ideas are capable of acceleration, even − hypothetically − unlimited growth.

There are common obstacles inevitably interrupting even the best of them.

You may know your strategy to become most highly valued by acquirers, partners, or investors, and what you need to do to be uniquely useful across the interconnected value chains. You have the makings of scalable success. Only the makings of it.

There can be risks in key personnel dependencies. Their accumulated know-how may be more critical than founders care to admit. Key value-adding differentiating activities are not easily repeatable, so consistency fails. Even cash injection can't overpower the inertia this causes. Scaling at all, never mind the notion of mainstreaming or reaching maximum scale, will imply a need to overcome this.

Just *a few use cases*, of processes, people, and technology, *underpin your success*. A few core processes, or use cases, need to work perfectly and possibly across third parties so that best outcomes are repeatable. It's critical to identify the few critical use cases and best practices that need repeatability. Then focus on the next steps to make these systematic for scale. NB: a CRM won't do this for you.

The thought process in achieving this is: 'I know what resulted in our best outcome. What now needs to happen repeatably? Who are key personas affecting success? What activities do I need from them? What visibility do they need from me? How do I adapt and automate systems my people use inconsistently? How do I drive compliance to achieve best outcomes?'

If you can't scale quickly enough, get help. The best opportunities are time-limited. You and your team have limitations. Your focus should remove constraints on accelerating to your endpoint, not worrying about whether your people can handle everything themselves. Operationalising externally could be the finishing touch to activate and ramp up activity quickly.

Become a mechanic

Success doesn't require blue-sky, transformation or re-engineering. I've always found mechanics is a better way of thinking. Smart people, checking the engine, knowing where to look and how to fine-tune, and course correcting step by step at the right times.

Breakthroughs are out there waiting to be won, and your work as chief business growth mechanic will help you win that race.

Steve Sanders is a go-to-market strategist, multiplying company level valuations. He integrates flair for unearthing breakthrough strategies with structured filtering for winning ideas, strengthening, and accelerating to market, achieving maximal performance with product, sales, marketing, delivery teams, by being systematically ready to scale.

Building businesses and rescuing others to multi-$Billions, Steve's evolved skills, method and style are embraced in startups and scaleups. Challenging norms of others, and himself, became a helpful habit. Thus, Steve deconstructs assumptions limiting potential, reforming for success in future horizons.

Nearly drowning in the Indian Ocean as a young man, Steve long held a fear of deep water. These days he's often in a sea kayak, striving to master SUP-boarding (for complete lack of balance) and experimenting with surf kayak and bodyboard. Living outside professional comfort zones and thriving, Steve applied this personally too, experiencing release from self-limitations, always going for breakthroughs.

linktr.ee/stevesanders

steve.sanders@businessgrowthmechanics.com

Plan The Work, Work The Plan

SUBASH TAVARES

In my career as a Chartered Civil Engineer, I have experienced both success and failure in the design and delivery of major programmes of work undertaken to improve the lives of people. At the core of the success is the mindset of the 'human factor' that underpins this delivery of not only major but complex programmes. Also, at the core are the lessons learned from the failures. I believe that this mindset is applicable to entrepreneurs, and in this chapter, I am going to share my thoughts as to how my mindset is applicable to the success of the entrepreneurs of the next generation[s]. It should be noted that in this chapter, the word 'project' is interchangeable and applicable to all market sectors and the delivery of all work delivered as a project, e.g. infrastructure, transformation, software development.

Plan the work

Scope of works: Although one would expect this as an obvious requirement, it is really important to examine this in detail. It is important to consider if the concept is viable, and in my sector, this is measured by the cost:benefit ratio, i.e. are the estimated costs proportionate to the derived benefits? For entrepreneurs, this is key, and in many cases, this is converting a 'gut feel' to reality.

Identify all stakeholders over the whole life cycle of the project: This is all about mapping all the stakeholders and the interdependencies. It is rare that stakeholders operate in a silo, and from my experience, the lack of management of the stakeholders can, and does, impact progress.

Costs: The estimated costs should be realistic. If not and the costs increase, then this would impact the cost:benefit ratio and potentially render the project unviable. However, there maybe philanthropic reasons to proceed, and as with all these issues, it is about having reliable data on which to make decisions.

Risks: Identify all risks to the delivery of the projects. There is a sense of inevitability that risks will impact, and the outturn costs will increase. However, if identified early and quantified, one can develop the appropriate mitigation plans to minimise or even remove the risk. It is often suggested that you need to spend money to make money! This may indeed be true, but good risk management can reduce your exposure – and who doesn't want to save money?

Plan the work (schedule): This is understanding all the activities required to deliver the project. These activities should then be considered in the sequence that they need to be done and the interdependencies with each other. This is important when 'approvals' are required by external bodies and the requisite time and costs associated with this.

Consider the ESG requirements: ESG (environmental, social and governance) criteria are of increasing interest to companies, their investors, and other stakeholders. With growing concern about the ethical status of quoted companies, these standards are the central factors that measure the ethical impact and sustainability of investment in a company. Although most people are aware of the carbon footprint, there are other important issues, i.e. sustainability, measures to achieve target zero, decommissioning [waste management]. These principles apply across all market sectors, and entrepreneurs need to be aware of their obligations. This is an emerging requirement, and I believe this will require constant review as it is both a legal and moral requirement. Examples of ESG are:

Environmental	Social	Governance
Waste and pollution	Employee relations and diversity	Tax strategy
Resource depletion	Working conditions	Executive remuneration
Greenhouse gas emission	Local communities	Donations and public lobbying
Climate change	Health and safety	Corruption and bribery
Deforestation	Conflict	Board diversity and structure

Work the plan

Manage change: As sure as eggs are eggs, there will always be change. The key here is to manage this in a structured way. My experience is that this is an area that is not valued. In many cases, this is because of the fear of upsetting the client. However, I believe that one should be building a relationship with the client/stakeholder to create an environment in which this can be discussed, evaluated, and resolved fairly. It is also my experience that change is requested and made prior to agreement as the associate impacts are not known.

Impact on cost, schedule, and quality: In my world, the key issues are cost, time, and quality and the aspiration is to have these three issues balanced. If one does not control all three proportionately, the outputs/ outcomes will be impacted. I would strongly recommend that whenever a change is requested, all three issues must be considered and signed off prior to incorporating the change. One must use their discretion when dealing with health and safety related issues.

Communication: Good, clear, unambiguous communication is very important to ensure that you bring all stakeholders and investors and, where appropriate, the customers on the journey.

Manage stakeholders: Identify, consult and manage all stakeholders. It should be noted that the stakeholders may change at different stages of the lifecycle, and this would be captured right at the beginning of the project – stakeholder mapping. The engagement of stakeholders must be planned to ensure that they are informed of what is required from them and when. My experience is that the importance of this is often underestimated.

Clear and accurate reporting: At all stages of the project life cycle, this is one of the most recognised forms of communication. This starts from the bottom up, and the requirements should be agreed right at the start of the project. It is true that as the report passes through the relevant hierarchy, it gets summarised, i.e. from detailed reports at the project delivery level to a 'one pager' at board level, or reporting by exception. Data is the basis from which all reporting is derived so it is my contention that it does need to be agreed right at the beginning and that all associated configurations are established. This will ensure that the data is not corrupted as it flows through the hierarchy. The most common issue with reporting is the interpretation of this data and the 'fear of reporting the truth'. In my experience, this is a cultural issue, and we all have a part to play in this. For entrepreneurs this is key in order to build confidence with potential clients, funders, and customers.

Close out and implement the product

Software, product, infrastructure: The principle here is about the client taking over the 'product' whatever the market sector. It might be suggested that the entrepreneur may not be responsible for the product once it is handed over to the client. It is my considered opinion that we all have a moral obligation to deliver the 'product' in a safe and usable state. It is true that contractual frameworks do 'muddy the waters' but this is to be addressed when considering the form of contract – at the core is the 'intent'.

Training (operational readiness, user manuals, including operation and maintenance manuals): In most instances, the post-contract conditions include the provision of training and/or support. It is my opinion that we should be including the end user right at the beginning of a project to ensure we understand their requirements and design the 'product' accordingly. There is also the need to consider how the 'product' will be integrated into the wider environment. This comes back to identifying all stakeholders, including operators, maintainer and end user.

Sustainable disposal: The disposal of all assets is now an important consideration, as per the ESG framework discussed earlier in this chapter. Designers are now responsible for the design, construction, safe operation and maintenance and decommissioning/disposal of all assets. Depending on the market sectors, the client/owners need to ensure that all these aspects are considered and approved at the relevant stage in the project life cycle. In the majority of cases, this role is delegated to a specialist body to assure compliance on behalf of the client/owner. My opinion is that entrepreneurs must be aware of these requirements, so they are addressed, usually starting by including these requirements in the contract.

Conclusion

As we come to the end of this chapter, and having considered my experience as a Chartered Civil Engineer, I hope that you, the reader, can see how the discipline/mindset one has is a transferable skill that transcends all market sectors. It is not always about doing things right, but rather doing the right thing. The balance here is the drive for financial gain (in itself not a bad thing) and the impact of what we do on the environment and all co-inhabitants on this planet.

Subash Tavares is a Chartered Civil Engineer and has +40 years of experience in engineering consultancy and programme/project management in the private sector working for Halliburton KBR, CH2MHILL and VINCI. His project experience has been gained mainly in water supply, water resources management and transportation infrastructure, including the delivery of projects and programmes from the concept/feasibility stage through to completion and handover.

In his early years, Subash worked in the design office, starting as Graduate Design Engineer and eventually promoted to Engineering Director at Haliburton/KBR. Over the last 15 years, Subash has gained significant experience in the programme management and controls of multi-disciplinary teams undertaking the detailed design and delivery of major complex programmes.

Subash is also a non-executive director for a major charity, Save the Children – his role is to provide strategic advisory services for temporary housing for children in crisis zones around the world, including Bangladesh, Turkey and Rwanda.

in www.linkedin.com/in/subash-f-j-tavares-ba34094

🌐 #subashtavares

f www.facebook.com/subash.tavares

The Right Money Mindset: A Necessity, Not A Nice-To-Have

LESLEY THOMAS

I believe that as an entrepreneur, having a successful business is 80% mindset and 20% strategy and having the right money mindset makes up the largest part of this.

Henry Ford said, 'If you think you can, or think you can't, you're right.' That really says it all. Whatever we tell ourselves is true for us becomes a self-fulfilling prophecy.

What is mindset?

Our mindset is quite simply the conversation we have with ourselves about our attitudes and beliefs. The official definition of mindset is 'The established set of attitudes held by someone'.

Mindset is made up of several key components:

- Thoughts

- Emotions

- Habits

- Strategies

- Beliefs

- History

- Values

- Shadows

- Experiences

- Memories

- Identity

Each of these components will feed into the conversation that is constantly going on in our head and will result in not only how we think about things but the actions we take or indeed don't take.

Your money mindset is a collection of beliefs about money, your perception about money, and here is the key part – it is intrinsically linked to your sense of self-value and self-worth.

This is why as entrepreneurs, it is vital to have the right mindset, and in particular, the right money mindset. Where mindset leads, business will follow. Money mindset will often be described in two ways, either an abundant mindset or a scarcity mindset. The former believes that there is no reason to be overly concerned about money, that it will be available when required and has the ability to attract more. Whereas in its simplest form, a scarcity mindset believes that there may never be enough money, that it is not easy to replace and therefore, what limited resources they have must be protected at all costs.

Our money mindset is the inner conversation we have with ourselves about money, our feelings about money and how those thoughts about money make us feel about ourselves.

It is widely accepted that our money mindset largely develops from childhood. As a result of our parent's relationship with money and how our parents spoke about money (and about people, with or without money) when we were children. You may have heard of the phrase, 'Give me the boy 'til seven and I will show you the man'. In other words, the formation of our beliefs and attitudes are well established by the time we are seven years old.

So how does a negative money mindset show up in business? There are many ways, and not all of them directly financial, but each will create a hit on your bottom line or your ability to increase the money you are making in your business.

These include:

- Over delivering and under-charging

- Not creating clear boundaries

- Either not setting goals, or making those goals too small to be impactful

- Shying away from conversations about money

- Holding prices the same for a long time

- Trading time for money

- Discounting unnecessarily

- Not tracking money into and out of the business daily

- Feeling negative thoughts or self-talk holding you back

- Not being visible enough in your business

- Not marketing yourself correctly – are you being loud and proud about what you do, who you do it for and the results you bring?

- Not niching down enough

These are all clear indicators of where someone's money mindset is not supporting them and where that sense of self-worth and self-value is actually sabotaging their business and professional success.

By understanding what is happening as a result of your money mindset, this is when you are able to take the action required to create the internal conversation that is supporting you and your goals and not self-sabotaging them. When you understand your money mindset and really understand your relationship with money, this is when you can see where the self-talk is a help and where it is a hindrance. When it's the latter, this can be the factor that is really preventing the success in your business that you are hoping for yet blaming 'poor strategy' for the results.

When you have the right relationship with money and, therefore, a supportive money mindset, so many aspects of yourself start to fall into place.

- You believe that you have no reason to compare yourself to others.

- You believe that you are capable of setting and achieving bold financial goals.

- You know how and when to spend your money, without guilt or compulsion.

- You are generous with your money and use it to help others.

- You accept your money story is yours alone (and not the one given to you by your parents).

- You believe that you are fully in charge of your own future.

- You never shy away from a conversation about money.

- You always know what your financial situation looks like.

- You feel empowered by money and not a slave to it.

- You see money as a tool to help you create the life you want to lead.

Time to be the change you want to see

We know that having a healthy relationship with money can help us feel more secure and confident in our lives, but what does that look like? How do we get there? And how do we stay on track once we start making progress? In fact, most people don't understand their own mindset when it comes to money and how that impacts the decisions they make every day.

You may feel like there's never enough money to go around. That there's too much month at the end of your money. You're not alone. In fact, many people are feeling the same way as you are right now. But it doesn't have to be this way.

Do you feel like your money mindset is holding you back? If so, it's time to understand how to change your relationship with money. You can learn the skills and tools that will help you make better decisions for yourself and your business. By understanding what drives your behaviour around money, you can take control of your finances instead of letting them control you.

We know that everyone has a different story about their relationship with money – some people love it, others hate it – but we all have one! Understanding where those feelings come from is key to changing our relationship with money for the better. It starts by learning more about yourself and your current relationship with money.

You don't need to be an expert to make your relationship with money better. To begin with, all it takes is asking yourself the right questions and making small changes in your daily life.

You can have the life that you've always wanted. It all starts with a few simple questions and some honest answers. The good news is, once you know what's going on, you can start making changes for the better. We just need to ask ourselves some tough questions about our relationship with money and then take action based on those answers. And if we do this right, this will create a framework and a methodology that can be applied time and time again.

By getting crystal clear on our current thoughts and feelings about money, this is how we can then create a plan to reset that relationship. Awareness that we have a problem or something getting in our way is the very first step in creating change.

Take a look at each of the questions below. Find a quiet space and consider each question carefully. Really feel what comes up for you. If it feels uncomfortable, lean into it. Journal out your response to each question – and be totally honest.

1. What do you feel when you think about money?

When answering this question, consider the following:

- What are you feeling?

- Is there a picture you form when you think of money?

- Is it a nice image or a negative image?

- In thinking about this question, are you feeling totally comfortable? If not, why not?

These are all clues and the first steps to rewiring your subconscious in a way that supports your relationship with money *and* empowers your relationship with money – which is the ultimate goal.

2. What is your current relationship with money?

Would you consider you have a healthy or unhealthy relationship with money? Do you feel you are in control or not in that relationship? Do you feel money has a positive or negative influence on your life right now?

3. How is this relationship affecting you and your business?

There are many ways that our relationship with money can affect our business. For example, if we have a negative association with money or fear of spending it, then we may be less likely to invest in the tools and resources needed for success. Or, if we're not clear on what financial goals we want to achieve through our business, then it will be difficult to make progress towards those goals. Our relationship with money has an impact on every aspect of our lives – including how much joy and fulfilment we experience from running a business.

4. How would you describe money?

Would you describe it as something nice maybe, a friend perhaps, something you have a strong affinity with, that you respect and welcome warmly into your life? Or do you have fewer positive feelings about money and see it as something to shy away from, something you don't want to think about and certainly don't like? Really think about your relationship with money and write down what comes up for you.

5. How would you feel about meeting money?

This is a really interesting question to help uncover those deeper feelings that you may not even be necessarily aware of. Would you give it a big warm hug? Would you shyly walk up and say hello? Would you hide from it and try and ensure it didn't see you?

6. On a scale of 1 to 10, how comfortable are you around money?

This a great one to be able to gauge your relationship with money in a measured way now, but also by asking yourself this question again in a few weeks' time.

7. How will your future self describe money in three words?

This is really important to place yourself and your relationship with money in the future. Being future focused removes you from where you are now and places you where you want to be. And helps you to create that connection and, over time, the change that you want to see for yourself. Starting with three little words...

What next?

Once you have considered each of these questions and journaled out the answers, you have the basic framework for improving that relationship. And more than this, you now have the baseline for where that relationship sits right now and a way to measure it going forward.

In creating this baseline, you have the opportunity now to really consider your current relationship with money, the impact that relationship is having on you and your business, and to proactively look at ways of improving it. Becoming aware of how you are talking internally to yourself about money is a start, and removing the negative language associated with your financial success is vital.

How we speak to ourselves about money is really the key to resetting our relationship with it. Learn to speak about money as though it were your best friend, a loyal supporter and someone significant in your life.

Then answer those six questions again in four weeks and see what comes up this time around. This is the key to creating a successful money mindset, which is working for you. Become really aware of the conversation you are having with yourself about money; therein lies the opportunity for change.

Lesley Thomas is an accredited Mindset and Money Breakthrough Business Coach, Sacred Money Archetype practitioner and host of the podcast *Let's Talk Money and More*. Known for her *Holistic Whole Business* approach to money make-overs, Lesley works with entrepreneurial women who under-charge, over-deliver and want to improve their relationship with money.

As she so aptly affirms, 'Doing what you love and being well-compensated for it only materialises once you've transformed your relationship with money.'

When Lesley is not creating powerful money make-overs for her clients, she can be found at her home in Wiltshire with her husband and two sons, treading the boards in her local village hall or accompanying her family to the Alps to indulge in their favourite outdoor pursuits (sshh, don't tell them she actually *hates* skiing – much preferring time in the Spa instead…).

🌐 linktr.ee/lesleythomascoaching

📘 www.facebook.com/groups/
thefinancialfreedomcollective (for female entrepreneurs)

You Are Probably Crazy...

MATT THOMPSETT

If you are seriously contemplating giving up your predictable, safe career to start your own business, you are probably crazy. Don't delude yourself. The odds of 'NewCo' surviving three years (around 1.5 million minutes of graft and sleep-annihilating anxiety) are 5%.

If NewCo survives, the chances of selling and achieving financial abundance are vanishingly small. Why are the odds so stacked against you? They are not. Actually, most newbies do the stacking themselves by not facing a few guileless truths.

I should know. In my 40+ years in business, I've made every mistake you can imagine and some you can't, some just once and some repeatedly until it hurt. So, take three truths from me that may just keep you from the abyss…

Assume your idea is dumb

Having a new business idea is like having a baby; no matter how it looks, you'll love it and dote on it with unconditional devotion. Every failed business has, at its core, a much-loved idea that the market coldly rejected. How do you avoid this? Simple, just assume your idea is dumb.

Let's look at some dumb ideas that cost their 'parents' dearly. The C5. Sir Clive Sinclair's brainchild that swiftly bankrupted everyone involved, leaving £7.75 million in debt. Assuming transcendent genius, Sir Clive conducted zero market research, failed to confer with industry experts (significantly after one such professional described the C5 as a 'ghastly mistake') and refused good council from his investors whenever his hypothesis and astonishing hubris was challenged. Sir Clive snubbed unanimously negative, early verdicts from motoring organisations, road safety groups, and consumer watchdogs. Even when the unstable C5 was condemned by the British Safety Council, the Dutch National Transport Service, the Automobile Association and Advertising Standards, Sir Clive refused to recognise his turkey. Did he ask himself, 'Will anyone pay a load of cash to wobble around for 30 minutes at 12 mph in a plastic shoe, exposed to rain and head-height, mortal collisions with SUV bonnets?'

How about the DeLorean? John DeLorean's fantasy that nose-dived into the ground in 1982, taking 2500 jobs and an eye-watering £200M of investment with it. The DeLorean was a poorly conceived entrant to an intensely competitive niche market with no pedigree and a challenging price tag. Again, DeLorean did zero consumer research. He rebuffed advice from the motor industry when told, 'there is simply no market for a stainless-steel bucket outperformed by a motor scooter'. He even convinced himself that the British Government would provide Export Credit financing to the tune of 80% of the cost of his dream car. That never happened. Perhaps he should have asked HM Government before playing with his spreadsheets? Did DeLorean ever ask himself, 'Will supercar enthusiasts pay well over the odds for a gull-winged, rust-proof tank that nudges 0-60 mph in eleven seconds?'

The message is simple, assume your idea is dumb, and you will test it to destruction before eating through your savings, losing your castle and having to plead for your old job back.

The test?

- Talk to a lot of informed people about your idea, not just family. I beg you, listen to feedback and focus on the critique, not the cooing.

- Identify and study potential competitors. There are always far more competitors than you imagine; can you differentiate your offering?

- Identify, with reliable data, the size of the potential market for your idea. Is it a rich and growing marketplace?

- Work with financial gurus to determine if there is enough market and margin for financial viability; remember NewCo must pay decent salaries and have predictable returns.

- Look at your idea through the lens of potential buyers, not your rose-tinted ones.

And the golden rule… listen most carefully to what you *don't* want to hear. Follow this advice, and I guarantee you will either save yourself from disaster or have a better planned and viable opportunity for success.

If you can't or won't sell, you are going to fail

I have worked with hundreds of bright, passionate innovators who simply cannot or will not sell. Some considered it 'dirty'; others find it impossible to ask for the deal. Trust me, if you won't or can't sell, you and your new business are doomed. From the day you even think of your venture, you must start selling – relentlessly.

Don't just think of selling as being in front of clenched-jawed buyers asking them to cough up for 10,000 of your left-handed, battery-powered nutcrackers; that's only part of the selling you will have to undertake.

You'll sell to hardened investors, banks, suppliers, job applicants, dependents, promoters, influencers and the market. You'll sell through your website, brand assets, presentations, face to face meetings, social media, press articles, resellers and a whole host of communication channels. You'll persuade strangers to invest in you, work for you, buy from you and promote you. You will be the 'eye of the storm', and you'll need to keep it that way, forever.

Understand what selling is. Selling is getting the outcome you want from interactions; agreement on a loan, acceptance of a job offer, contract to supply, a profitable order and so on. Regardless, selling always follows the same basic rule.

To close a 'deal', you must assure value that meets or exceeds the expectations of the 'buyer'. Think of a loan. For the bank to agree to your loan, you must meet their criteria of low-risk, security and collectable interest. If not, it will be a no, disdainful of how effervescent you are about your 'next best thing'.

Likewise, for a supplier to work with you, you need to be credible (accent on credit), with volume and security. Footnote; most newbies don't appreciate that suppliers on 30-day terms are making a loan (albeit in goods rather than cash), so treat them like an investor.

When it comes to selling your product or service, no one ever cares what 'it' does – only what 'it' will do for them.

Features of your product or service are irrelevant unless your buyer can clearly see the benefits to them, personally. Spend significantly more time questioning and listening, don't spout on and on about your offering.

An example. I had a call from a Java Technology recruitment company last week, nice chap called Simon. Simon exhausted twenty minutes lecturing me about his company, their processes, track record, referrals and so on. He didn't ask me one question apart from his over-familiar 'Hi Matt, how are you today, mate?' Simon proudly announced that 'new customers get 25% discount off normal rates' – genius! As he gasped for oxygen, I told him we are a 'low-code' development company, and we never have and never will have any use whatsoever, ever, for Java developers. Perhaps he should have asked me what technologies we use before his well-practised marketing narrative. Sorry Simon, better luck elsewhere!

Fundamentally, get to know your 'buyer' first. What they value, what they need, what they buy, what pain or challenges they have and what solutions they seek. Do this and discover how you might meet and exceed their expectations. Selling takes a lot of questioning and careful listening to shape your pitch. Remember, when you hit all the right buttons, ask for the deal...

Learn to sell.

If you think you understand finance, think again

Excel is not truth. I know you have a neat spreadsheet that 'forecasts' a relentless climb from startup to breakeven to challenging Elon Musk's primacy on the rich list. But I also know there are five critical formulas you haven't built into cells B35-D62.

1. The first most common omission is the entrepreneur's salary. Paying yourself nothing or a pittance from the get-go is bizarrely common and equally stupid. If your predictions mean you can't pay yourself at least a modest living wage, you are creating an artificial business. Bet your last Krugerrand this will cause you more trauma than you can imagine, and it means your model is fundamentally flawed. No bank will respect your business plan if you have no income, they have seen that before, and it 100% never turns out well. Either your market capture is not viable, or your startup capital is too low. Get real.

2. The second most common omission is not pessimistically sensitising your cash cycles. You will be paid significantly later than you think, so don't plan on 30 days for invoice payment; use 90 days and cross your fingers. Poor incoming cashflow is the most common cause of failure, second to having a dumb idea (re-read section one). As for outgoing cash, assume everything will cost you a

lot more by adding 25-30% contingency on every expenditure item, including salaries, bean bags and frothy coffee makers.

3. By sprinkling a little harsh reality on your spreadsheet, it's not so perfect now, is it? Re-examine your idea and ask yourself the 'dumb' question. Usually, what it means is that your estimate for startup cash is way short, and you should rethink how you finance your 'next best thing'. It may be telling you 'don't do it', it will unquestionably help you to avoid early cash-starvation by having a robust plan that represents worst case. Critically, your bank and investors will love it.

4. If you make it past 'spreadsheet reality', secure your financing and get going, remind yourself every hour of every day that cash is king. No matter how well things get going, do not start salivating over supercars or designer watches; drive a 2005 Prius and ask Siri for the time. Work from your shed and borrow/beg everything you can; ignore fabulously appointed serviced office space until there are no garden chairs left to sit your team on. Spend your cash only on stuff or services that make or save money, increase production, create markets and generate sales.

5. Do not give away equity unless you have zero other choices; keep your shares in a vicious headlock.

If you need to get them back for any reason in the future, it will be tough and expensive. Shares in your startup today are probably worthless, but in a few years, with providence and vigilant management, they could be surprisingly valuable. If you have scattered shares like confetti, you will have cheerfully diluted your control and value. When shareholders quit or get fired, you will spend a fortune getting the shares back as those exiting use maximum leverage.

6. Finally, don't discount. Remember Simon? He offered me 25% off. I hadn't asked. If Simon's gross margin is 40%, he didn't give away 25%; he gave away 62.5% of his profit. Discount reduces the sale price not the cost price! You have done your research, formulated your costs accurately and built your target margin into your business plan, hence your price stands. You get asked for a discount when you have not correctly positioned your offering, such that the buyer understands exactly the benefits and value multiplier it will bring to them. Resist.

Standing on the edge of the abyss, chewing broken glass

I am certain I have shared enough to make you think twice about starting your own business, which I am equally certain you will ignore. Good for you! Undoubtedly, the prevalent driver for entrepreneurs is not the idea itself but the aspiration to self-determination, freedom of choice and reaping the rewards of your 'next best thing'. Having your own business is not like that. Not until your business literally thrives, and for most entrepreneurs, not even then. You will be working countless hours, chewing your fingernails to your elbows over potential deals, fretting over every penny in and out, sweating over month-end figures and watching the family going off on holiday without you.

Make no mistake, every day will feel like standing on the edge of the abyss, chewing broken glass. Will it fail and fall into the abyss? Only if you let it. What about all the things you must do that you really don't wish to? Chew that glass! After 40+ years, I wouldn't have it any other way; good luck...

Matt Thompsett is a self-confessed expert in avoiding and surviving colossal screw-ups in business. Matt is founder and Chief Vision Officer for a fast-growing technology business; Green Lemon Company builds systems and AI solutions for customers from Central Government to Financial Services. His vision for Green Lemon Company is to 'Harness technology for the benefit of every species on the planet'. Matt is currently swinging the business to focus on purpose rather than profit, working as a member of the UN Global Compact to support the UN Sustainable Development Goals.

Matt's journey has taken him from Forestry to Sales, Sales & Management Training to Recruitment and Technology 'with countless mistakes and good fortune along the way…'. Matt privately mentors new business owners to help others avoid the pitfalls and build viable businesses. In his spare time, he is studying for his BSc (Hons) in Environmental Science.

🌐 www.greenlemoncompany.net

in www.linkedin.com/in/mattthompsett

🐦 www.twitter.com/greenlemonmatt